MW00633089

ut though my feelings were deep and often poignant, still I kept

I became somewhat partial to the Methodist sect, and I felt so

son young as I was, and so unacquainted with men and things,

ians were most decided against the Baptists and Methodists, and used all the powers of both reaso

hand; the Baptists and Methodists in their turn were equally zealous in endeavoring to establish th

e? Who of all these parties are right; or, are they all wrong together? If any one of them be rig

t, I was one day reading the Epistle of James, first chapter and fifth verse, which reads: If any

ll be given him.

s time to mine. It seemed to enter with great force into every feeling of my heart. I reflected on

t know, and unless I could get more wisdom than I then had, I would never know; for the teach

confidence in settling the question by an appeal to the Bible.

must do as James directs, that is, ask of God. I at length came to the determination to "ask of Go

d, I might venture.

attempt. It was on the morning of a beautiful, clear day, early in the spring of eighteen hundred a

I had never as yet made the attempt to pray vocally.

and finding myself alone, I kneeled down and began to offer up the desires of my heart to God.

d had such an astonishing influence over me as to bind my tongue so that I could not speak. Th

had seized upon me, and at the very moment when I was ready to sink into despair and abandon mys

d, who had such marvelous power as I had never before felt in any being—just at this moment of gr

radually until it fell upon me.

the light rested upon me I saw two Personages, whose brightness and glory defy all descrip

e other—This is My Beloved Son. Hear Him!

During this time of great excitement my mind was called up to serious reflection and great uneasin...

...ugh I attended their several meetings as often as occasion would permit. In process of time my...

...reat were the confusion and strife among the different denominations, that it was impossible for a...

...s right and who was wrong.

My mind at times was greatly excited, the cry and tumult were so great and incessant. The Pres...

...d sophistry to prove their errors, or, at least, to make the people think they were in error. On the o...

...n tenets and disprove all others.

In the midst of this war of words and tumult of opinions, I often said to myself: What is to b...

...ich is it, and how shall I know it?

While I was laboring under the extreme difficulties caused by the contests of these parties of religio...

... lack wisdom, let him ask of God, that giveth to all men liberally, and upbraideth not; and i...

Never did any passage of scripture come with more power to the heart of man than this did a...

...in and again, knowing that if any person needed wisdom from God, I did; for how to act I di...

...religion of the different sects understood the same passages of scripture so differently as to destroy a...

At length I came to the conclusion that I must either remain in darkness and confusion, or els...

...cluding that if he gave wisdom to them that lacked wisdom, and would give liberally, and not up...

So, in accordance with this, my determination to ask of God, I retired to the woods to make...

...enty. It was the first time in my life that I had made such an attempt, for amidst all my anxi...

After I had retired to the place where I had previously designed to go, having looked around...

...d scarcely done so, when immediately I was seized upon by some power which entirely overcame m...

...rkness gathered around me, and it seemed to me for a time as if I were doomed to sudden destructio...

But, exerting all my powers to call upon God to deliver me out of the power of this enemy whi...

...o destruction—not to an imaginary ruin, but to the power of some actual being from the unseen...

...rm, I saw a pillar of light exactly over my head, above the brightness of the sun, which descend...

It no sooner appeared than I found myself delivered from the enemy which held me bound. W...

...anding above me in the air. One of them spake unto me, calling me by name and said, pointing t...

HEAR HIM

Front cover: *Road to Emmaus* by Wendy Keller; *Let Not Your Hearts Be Troubled* by Howard Lyon; *Early Spring 1820* by Jeffery R Pugh; *Beacon of Light* Jen Tolman; *Every Knee Shall Bow* by J. Kirk Richards; *Gethsemane's Path* by Steve McGinty; *Man of Sorrows* by Paul Grass

Back cover: *If Any of You Lack Wisdom* by Linda Curley Christensen; *Tangible Light* by Sam Newton; *Jesus el Cristo* by Jorge Cocco Santángelo; *To the Rescue* by Robert A. Boyd; *Prince of Peace* by Lynne Millman-Weidinger; *I Have Succored Thee* by Mary Brickey

Cover and interior design by Michelle Fryer
Art direction by Margaret L. Weber
Production design by Natalie Brown, Kimberly Kay, Christina Marcano, and Aleesa Parsons
Cover design copyright © 2020 by Covenant Communications, Inc.

Published by Covenant Communications, Inc.
American Fork, Utah

Copyright © 2020 Covenant Communications, Inc
All rights reserved. No part of this book may be reproduced in any format or in any medium without the written permission of the publisher, Covenant Communications, Inc., 1226 South 630 East, Suite 4, American Fork, UT 84003. This material is neither made, provided, approved, nor endorsed by Intellectual Reserve, Inc. or The Church of Jesus Christ of Latter-day Saints. Any content or opinions expressed, implied or included in or with the material are solely those of the owner and not those of Intellectual Reserve, Inc. or The Church of Jesus Christ of Latter-day Saints.

Printed in China

First Printing: October 2020

26 25 24 23 22 21 20   10 9 8 7 6 5 4 3 2 1

ISBN 978-1-52440-291-4

HEAR HIM

Contents

The Lord's Prayer by Darren Gygi

Introduction

BY MARGARET L. WEBER

It is easy to say that 2020 has been unlike any other year in my fifty plus years of life. I daresay most of you will understand that without need of further explanation. But for me, even while it has been difficult, it has also been profoundly rewarding.

I have been the art director at Covenant Communications for the past twenty-two years. I love my work and am honored and blessed to interact with gifted artists, photographers, designers, authors, and speakers daily. For the last few years, I have wanted to create a book that would showcase the talent of the wonderful visual artists who portray the Savior and His life's story in every medium. In the middle of 2018, I began reviewing images and contacting artists I wished to include in such a project. The artists' names and potential art were relatively easy to compile, but I struggled to decide what text should accompany the imagery. With such beautiful portrayals of the Savior and His life and ministry, the text needed to be something truly inspired and inspiring. Several people suggested ideas that I considered, but the right text was elusive, and the book remained on the list of uncompleted projects throughout 2019 and into the beginning of 2020.

Like so much of 2020, April's general conference set a precedent. President Russell M. Nelson had asked us to prepare for a conference like no other. "General conference next April will be different from any previous conference. In the next six months, I hope that every member and every family will prepare for a unique conference that will commemorate the very foundations of the restored gospel" ("Closing Remarks," *Ensign*, Nov. 2019). In an effort to heed his counsel, I did some reading to refresh my knowledge and understanding of Joseph Smith's First Vision and felt reasonably prepared. But now, because general conference was occurring during a worldwide pandemic, there would be no gathering of the Saints to the Conference Center on Temple Square in Salt Lake City or even to stake and ward buildings. And since I live alone, this meant a few days to very privately listen to the revelations and inspirations from the living prophet and Apostles. Facing some personal trials and amid the chaotic nature of the current world climate, I listened with an unusual fervor.

First Vision by Stacy Weitz Minch

Christ in America by CCA Christensen

Shortly after conference, I had the opportunity to speak with the author Michael Wilcox. To say that Michael is well read would be an understatement. In our occasional conversations, I have found him to have a keen mind, a gentle spirit, and a broad understanding of many subjects. And as we discussed the recent conference and our personal take on the messages, I had new insight as Michael enumerated the pattern of the message of Joseph's First Vision:

1. Joseph heard, "This is My Beloved Son. Hear Him!"—some of the first words uttered to anyone in this dispensation were a personal call to Joseph using his actual name, with a directive to hear Christ—we have been commanded to Hear Him (Joseph Smith—History 1:17).

2. Christ spoke to Joseph, saying, "Joseph, my son, thy sins are forgiven thee"—this acknowledged that Joseph, who desired forgiveness, received mercy—Christ readily forgives our sins (*The Joseph Smith Papers, Journal, 1835–1836;* josephsmithpapers.org/paper-summary/journal-1835-1836/25).

3. And finally, Christ told Joseph to "go not after [any church]"—Joseph asked a question of God and received an answer, learning that he should not join

Jesus the Christ by T.R. Larsen

Silent Night
by Debbie Wood

any church because a restoration of the fulness of the gospel was needed—Christ hears our prayers and can answer our questions (*The Joseph Smith Papers*, "*Church History, 1 March 1842 [Wentworth Letter],*" *Circa 1838 History*; josephsmithpapers.org/articles/primary-accounts-of-first-vision).

For me, every conference message fit perfectly into this simple synopsis. And finally the desired text for this book became clear in my mind, and I knew with a surety that this was the message meant to be paired with the incredible imagery of our Lord and Savior. It all resonated in perfect harmony, a masterful orchestration. And isn't that how it often sounds when we Hear Him?

During the next few weeks, as more than two dozen authors wrote under a very demanding deadline, I contacted the artists for their images of Christ. Ultimately, more than two hundred talented individuals contributed their inspired art of the life and service of the Savior. With so many participants, we could use only one piece from each gifted artist.

In the pages that follow, you will find art that represents the Savior's humble birth, His sinless life, and many parts of His inspiring ministry. You will see portrayals of His great atoning sacrifice and even His resurrected glory. And

The Plan of Salvation by Matthew Hyrum Dell

I have learned that when the promptings of the Holy Ghost come to us, we are literally hearing what the Lord desires us to hear.

—ELDER GARY E. STEVENSON

Living Water by Barbara Summers Edwards

you will identify works that testify of the First Vision and the fulness of the gospel's Restoration. All of these images sit alongside the authors' testimonials of the Savior, who reaches out in a very personal way to each of His Father's sons and daughters as they work through their individual tests and trials.

In February 2020, President Nelson issued a special invitation: "I invite you to think deeply and often about this key question: How do *you* hear Him? I also invite you to take steps to hear Him better and more often" ("President Nelson's Second Invitation of 2020: 'How Do You Hear Him? #HearHim'"; churchofjesuschrist.org/church/news/president-nelsons-second-invitation-of-2020-how-do-you-hear-him-hearhim?lang=eng). This book was created for that very purpose.

Intercession by Stacey Abts

I am so grateful for those who contributed to this book's creation through word and art. My cup has been filled to overflowing by their good works. And I add my testimony to theirs of our Savior and His divine life. It is my experience that Heavenly Father and Jesus Christ know and love each of us personally. I pray that you might discern Christ's voice and feel His love in the words and images of this book as you seek to Hear Him.

Abide with Me, 'Tis Eventide by Kristin Yee

Pray through the Darkness

BY S. MICHAEL
WILCOX

What I love most about Joseph Smith's accounts of the First Vision is the beauty of a boy seeking his Father, described in simple, powerful, and relevant words that direct our own efforts at communing with Heaven. Even more than the mature prophet of Nauvoo, it is the bewildered boy searching for his God that draws Joseph Smith so deeply into my heart. I will focus on just three thoughts from that world-changing event that have comforted and guided me throughout life.

Joseph described himself in the 1838 account of the First Vision as "an obscure boy . . . a boy of no consequence in the world" (Joseph Smith—History 1:22). There is such endearing humility here! The eminent bridging significance of his entire life is the assertion that God speaks to obscure boys and girls. Such am I—as obscure as you can find. Such are we all. He is a revealing God—a God who wishes his children to Hear Him. Church voices—from parents, who

First Vision by Downy Doxey-Marshall

The Lord Opened the Heavens by Nancy Andruk Olson

Brothers and sisters, how can we become the men and women—the Christlike servants—the Lord needs us to be? How can we find answers to questions that perplex us? If Joseph Smith's transcendent experience in the Sacred Grove teaches us anything, it is that the heavens are open and that God speaks to His children.

—PRESIDENT RUSSELL M. NELSON

teach us to pray, to conference talks to missionaries to primary choristers—affirm this opening truth from the boy prophet. "Heavenly Father, are you really there? And do you hear and answer ev'ry child's prayer?" ("A Child's Prayer," *Children's Songbook*, 12). Joseph said of God on that spring morning, "If he gave wisdom to them that lacked wisdom . . . I might venture" (Joseph Smith—History 1:13). Harold Bloom, America's scholar and foremost literary critic, spoke of "Joseph Smith's heroic enterprise in lessening the distance between God and man" (Harold Bloom, *The American Religion*, [New York: Chu Hartley Publishers], 1992, 108). Now more than two centuries since the Sacred Grove, Joseph's words testify to me, "You might venture too." A fourteen-year-old boy's prayer in 1820 thus began for me a lifetime of talking with my Father in Heaven.

But sometimes we have to pray through the darkness before the pillar of light appears—pray when we are at the edge of "despair"—at the "moment of great alarm" (Joseph Smith—History 1:16). Then we Hear Him. That is also one of the first great lessons of the Restoration! The young Joseph, in the grove, believing he would get an answer but overcome with darkness, prayed through it, "exerting all [his] powers to call upon God to deliver [him] . . . and at the very moment when [he] was ready to sink into despair . . . just at this moment of great alarm, [he] saw a pillar of light" (Joseph Smith—History 1:16). There is something good, mandated even, about exerting all our powers when surrounded by forces with "such an astonishing influence" (Joseph Smith—History 1:15). We pray through the darkness until the light appears. This has happened more than once in my life—light living in darkness, breaking through it! Tennyson once wrote:

And Power was with him in the night,
Which makes the darkness and the light,
And dwells not in the light alone.

(Alfred Lord Tennyson, "In Memoriam A. H. H.
OBIIT MDCCCXXXIII: 96.")

But the most beloved truth of 1820 for me is the import of that first encouragement—command, if you wish—of the Restoration, issuing from the Father's own lips—just two words: "Hear Him!" What does the Father desire us to hear, perhaps above all other things? Joseph was seeking forgiveness among the trees that morning. "I cried unto the Lord for mercy, for there was none else to whom I could go and obtain mercy" (Joseph Smith, "Circa Summer 1832 History," churchofjesuschrist. org/study/manual/first-vision-accounts/1832-

Tree of Life
by Robert McKay

account?lang=eng). The Father's introductory words, "This is My Beloved Son. Hear Him!", were an invitation to receive what the Son brings to all— *Forgiveness!* "Joseph, my son, thy sins are forgiven thee" (Joseph Smith, "Circa Summer 1832") were the first words Joseph heard. In our need for forgiveness, the Father lovingly says, "Hear Him!" It is the beginning of our history. The Restoration commences with mercy offered to all obscure boys and girls who pray through darkness. Joseph said of that moment of compassion so universal in its application, "My soul was filled with love, and for many days I could rejoice with great joy" (Joseph Smith, "Circa Summer 1832"). The forgiving light of the Father and Son "filled me with joy unspeakable" (Joseph Smith, "Journal, 9–11, November 1835"). One of the verifying confirmations of truth is accompanying love and joy.

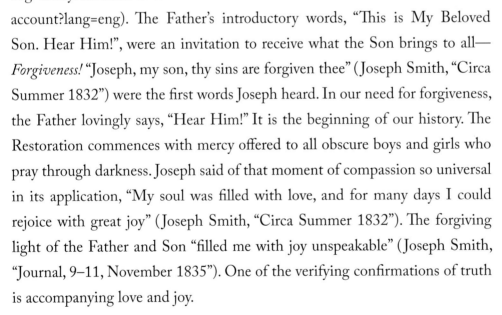

His prayer answered, Joseph returned home and told his mother the most important eight words I believe he ever spoke. "All is well . . . I have learned for myself" (Joseph Smith—History 1:20). Joseph Smith teaches us we can learn for ourselves and that all can be well—that all is well. Pray through the darkness! God reveals! God is forgiving! Hear Him! At the tomb of Lazarus,

Christ in Red Robe by Gary Earnest Smith

We have a vast history in art of those who have attempted to paint the Savior. Artists, through the ages, all seem to have the same objective in trying to find the spiritual qualities of the Christ, as wide and varied as they are. I typically don't use models for my Savior paintings. I start with a feeling and work toward it. From the beginning to the end, I go through experimentation—work and rework. One painting of my interpretation of Christ's face took sixteen years to complete. We artists often look for vindication of how our Christ images have positive effects on those who view the work. We seriously strive to seek His face (see Psalms 27:8), as we are admonished in the scriptures. Painting or sculpting the Savior's image is one of the most challenging and noble of artistic pursuits.

—GARY ERNEST SMITH

Come Forth by Richard Lance Russell

The Savior and Mary by Ben McPherson

Jesus offered a simple prayer: "Father, I thank thee that thou hast heard me. And I knew that thou hearest me always" (John 11:41–42).

Here is the answer to most prayers—the knowledge we are heard, that we might venture. This is true especially when we "[cry] unto the Lord for mercy" (Joseph Smith, "Circa Summer 1832"), as the young Joseph Smith knew.

Beacon of Light by Jen Tolman

Christ Smiling by Ken Corbett

He Calmed the Sea by Carol Merrill-Flitton

A Reminder of His Love

BY JEN TOLMAN

In college, I wanted to be a religious painter; however, a few of my teachers raised the question of whether it was even okay to represent Christ in paintings since we didn't know what He looked like. They wondered how an artist would attempt to depict someone so holy. I felt more confused then ever about what was okay and what was not. I decided it was safer to leave the subject alone.

For years afterward, I did not hang pictures of Christ in our home. But in time, I had two experiences that changed my mindset.

I became chronically ill and was basically bedridden for a time. During my pain and hardship, I felt the desire to have paintings of Christ all around me, like someone who was thirsting for water. I must have had at least four or five prints of Jesus in the room with me. They were reminders that He was there every second of my pain. I wondered why I felt so much peace and comfort

The Savior by Albin Veselka

from them if they couldn't be accurate. But they helped me so much during that struggle.

Months later, my very young child gave me a picture he had drawn of me. It obviously did not depict me in the least. It was a stick figure with long legs coming out of a circle-shaped body connected to a head with no neck. My hair probably looked more like a frizzled mop than a real head of hair, but this drawing made me extremely happy! I loved it so much that I hung it up on my

The more I can hear Him, the more of an effective instrument I will be to bring others to that same love that I feel. If I can learn to hear Him, to hear His voice, to hear His Spirit, then I can handle the challenges that come my way.

—SISTER JEAN B. BINGHAM

refrigerator for everyone to see. In that instant, I felt God saying to my soul, "This is how I feel when you paint me. I am so delighted about the artwork you create of me. I love it!"

Love's Pure Light by Erin Morton

I could picture Him holding one of my paintings of Him, I being the young child who was lovingly trying to depict my parent in the best way I could. My painting may not have been an accurate depiction of Him, but He beamed with joy at how hard I had worked to create it for Him. Then He lovingly hung it up for everyone to see. He wanted *everyone* to see it. He was so proud, and it made Him happy.

I later thought, *Wouldn't that be one of the best lies Satan would try to spread?* "Don't paint pictures of Christ. You don't know what He looks like. You don't have your facts or history right. You can't paint Him accurately. He is too holy for you to paint— just don't even go there."

No one would have pictures of Him in their homes.

No reminders. Less thoughts of Him.

Makes so much sense. As I've felt Christ encourage me, I've painted Him to remind others of Him, to help remind them of the feeling of Him, that He is there. To remind them of His light and love and joy.

When personal difficulty, doubt, or discouragement darken our path, or when world conditions beyond our control lead us to wonder about the future, the spiritually defining memories from our book of life are like luminous stones that help brighten the road ahead, assuring us that God knows us, loves us, and has sent His Son, Jesus Christ, to help us return home.

—ELDER NEIL L. ANDERSEN

Paintings of Christ, or paintings that include Christ, usually, if not always have as their true subject an important message that the artist is trying to share. Since I don't know what Christ looked like or looks like, I naively assume that the message is what the viewer will be concerned with as well, not the physical appearance or features of the Christ figure in the image. The first time I painted an image of Christ for the Church it was rejected. The reason given was that His countenance or the feeling projected was wrong, no mention was made of the physical appearance. I have used that as my guide since then.

—WALTER RANE

Christ and Children by Walter Rane

Be Ye Followers of Me by Naomi Brown

The Master's Call

BY EMILY BELLE
FREEMAN

I come from a long line of shepherds. My father wanted us to understand this part of our heritage, so as we were growing up our family kept a small flock of sheep. One of the sheep I will never forget had the name of "Big Mama." She earned this title because she was the leader of the flock.

Each spring brought changes to the flock as new lambs were born and older lambs would be sold, but Big Mama remained a constant. She loved my dad. It did not matter where she was on the one-acre patch of ground where we kept the sheep, when she heard him call she would come running. She had a very uncommon bleat, and my dad could mimic it exactly. And so he would call, and she would answer, and when she came, the rest of the flock would follow.

One morning my dad woke me up early and said that the sheep had gone missing. They had found a hole in the fence and had wandered off. My dad had already driven through the surrounding streets but had not seen them anywhere. He had concluded that they must have wandered through the fields and joined a flock of more than one hundred other sheep about a mile away from our home.

He wanted me to come with him to talk to the farmer and to see if we could retrieve our sheep.

The farmer was not pleased to see my father. Our sheep were not marked, and unfortunately, neither were his. My dad tried to explain that his sheep would come when he called, and the farmer just shook his head.

Finding the One
by Matt Warren

My dad climbed up on the tailgate of our old white truck and started to bleat. I wish you could have seen the look on that farmer's face. The first and second calls were followed by silence. I have to admit I was a little worried. I wondered how important my dad would be to Big Mama now. But my dad wasn't worried—he kept calling. And finally, from the back corner of the field there was the familiar reply. My dad repeated the call loudly and consistently as

Big Mama made her way through the huge flock, followed by our other lambs. The farmer watched in amazement and then helped us load our sheep into the back of the truck so that we could take them home.

In John Chapter 10, Christ taught the parable of the good shepherd. To fully understand this parable it is important for us to understand how a shepherd of that time period would care for his sheep. "In the East the flocks are at night driven into a large fold, and charge of them is given to an under-shepherd . . . when the shepherd comes in the morning, 'the doorkeeper' or 'guardian' opens to him. Having thus gained access to his flock . . . the shepherd knows and

The One by Chad Winks

The One by Justine Peterson

calls them, each by his name, and leads them out. Then the Eastern shepherd places himself at the head of his flock, and goes before them, guiding them, making sure of their following simply by his voice, which they know" (AE, Vol. II, 189–90).

Christ said of Himself, "I am the good shepherd: the good shepherd giveth his life for the sheep" (John 10:11). As the Good Shepherd, He has promised

Well Pleased by Kalene Walker

to lead us, protect us, heal us, defend us, and comfort us. He gave His life for us. In return He asks each of us to "come, follow me" (Luke 18:22). But to follow Him we must know His voice. In a world filled with confusion and commotion it can be hard to recognize the voice of the Shepherd. Elder Dallin H. Oaks has said, "From among the chorus of voices we hear in mortality, we must recognize the voice of the Good Shepherd, who calls us to follow him toward our heavenly home" ("Alternate Voices," *Ensign*, May 1989, 27).

The voice of the Shepherd can be heard in many different ways. It may be the still, small voice of the Holy Ghost that gently guides and prompts. Sometimes it is the clarion call from the prophet of the Lord, setting a clear standard by which we can direct our lives. Often it is the sure and steady witness of the scriptures that encourages us and increases our ability to recognize the voice of the Lord.

Faith by Trent Gudmundsen

Seeking the One by Liz Lemon Swindle

The sheep is worthy of divine rescue simply because it is loved by the shepherd.

—ELDER DIETER F. UCHTDORF

When I paint, I always start with the eyes because they are the soul of each painting. Each day as I came into the studio while working on *Seeking the One*, I had an overwhelming feeling that He was looking at me. Some days, I did not feel comfortable looking into His eyes and avoided them, knowing I could do more or be more than I was. Other days, I felt comfortable around Him and drew great strength by looking into His eyes.

As the painting neared completion, I started showing it to others, and I was amazed to find that they had the same reaction I did. Some people did not want to look into His eyes, others smiled, and some cried. It was then I realized that He was not only looking for me but that He was also looking for all of us. I remembered His words, "What man of you, having an hundred sheep, if he lose one of them, doth not leave the ninety and nine, and go after that which is lost?" (Luke 15:4). I realized we are each lost in our own way and that the Good Shepherd never stops seeking after us until He has found us and carried us home—until we Hear Him.

—LIZ LEMON SWINDLE

To know the voice of the Shepherd is a privilege and a blessing. Setting aside time to listen to the voice is our responsibility. We show our devotion to the Shepherd when we choose to listen to His voice and to come when we are called. His concerned and consistent call will beckon to us daily. It is up to us to quickly answer, "I'm coming!" For "if a man bringeth forth good works he hearkeneth unto the voice of the good shepherd, and he doth follow him" (Alma 5:41).

Sometimes we may find ourselves lost in a world of uncertainty. With so many concerns vying for our attention we may not hear the whisper of the still, small voice, we may not have time to seek out the clarion call, and we may set aside the sure and steady instruction from the scriptures.

In those tender moments we must remember that there is One who has set aside everything to seek us. He will not rest until He knows that we have heard His voice and we find ourselves nestled safely in His arms.

This essay is modified from *Closer to Christ* by Emily Belle Freeman, 2018 © Deseret Book Company. Used with permission.

The Sure Word of the Father

BY JOHN W. WELCH

No message could be more important for all people to hear than this one. On three momentous occasions in the history of the world, God the Father spoke the words **"This is my beloved Son: Hear Him" (Mark 9:7)**: as He introduced His Son to Joseph Smith in 1820; as He addressed Peter, James, and John at the Transfiguration of Jesus (see Matthew 17:5); and as Jesus came to the temple in Bountiful, where survivors had gathered (see 3 Nephi 11). Each of these instances teaches us how the Father would like us to hear Jesus. In his First Vision, Joseph listened personally and privately. From the

Joseph's Prayer Opened Heaven by Sarah Richards Samuelson

Transfiguration, we learn to hear through priesthood channels. And as with the people at Bountiful, we Hear Him collectively as His covenant community.

Hearing Him Privately

Joseph Smith spoke often about his First Vision. Several accounts mention the words of the Father in particular. In 1835, Joseph preached a sermon on the subject of the words "This is My Beloved Son. Hear Him" (see William W. Phelps to Sally Phelps, June 2, 1835, MS, Church History Library, Salt Lake City, UT).

Heard Me by Jessica Michaelson

In 1838, Joseph recorded: "One of them spake unto me, calling me by name, and said, pointing to the other—This is my Beloved Son. Hear Him!" (Joseph Smith—History 1:17). On August 28, 1843, David Nye White, editor of the Pittsburgh Weekly Gazette, reported things Joseph had told him, including: "Directly I saw a light, and then a glorious personage in the light, and then another personage, and the first personage said to the second, 'Behold, this is my beloved Son, hear him'" (John W. Welch, *Opening the Heavens: Accounts of Divine Manifestations 1820–1844* [Provo: BYU Studies, 2005], 25). And on May 24, 1844, Alexander Neibaur, a recently arrived convert in Nauvoo, recorded: "Br Joseph tolt us . . . saw a fire towards heaven[,] came near & nearer[,] saw a personage . . . [who said] *"this is my Beloved son harken ye him"* (Welch, *Opening the Heavens*, 26, italics added, original spelling).

Where Learning Takes Place by Simon Winegar

From the Prophet Joseph's experience, we can learn much about hearing the Lord. Joseph heard Him when he was alone. We too can take private time to leave the ways of the world behind and open our spiritual ears that we might hear and our hearts that we might understand.

Joseph had been taught by righteous parents and the scriptures. Planting and nurturing the word of God in our minds prepares our souls to perceive and resonate with the mind and will of Christ, to hear and recognize when He is speaking to us.

Joseph had pressing questions. He took time out of his regular routine to focus on matters of eternal importance and took his requests to God. He willingly sought and accepted personal direction. He sincerely desired forgiveness. Because he was ready to say in his heart, "Not my will, but thine be done," Joseph heard Him.

And then Joseph shared his experience, testifying of what he had heard. One way to hear more is to speak up, magnifying each gift we are given by helping others.

Hearing Him Authoritatively

These words were also heard by Peter, James, and John on the Mount of Transfiguration as recorded in Matthew 17:1–9, Mark 9:2–10, and Luke 9:28–36. Though not exactly the same, these three accounts are in harmony with each other. They teach us more about hearing Him.

Jesus took these three Apostles with him into a mountain to pray (see Luke 9:28). Entering the House of the Lord is one way of going into the "the hill of the Lord" (Psalms 24:3) to hear His word. As Jesus was transfigured, his "face did shine as the sun, and his raiment was white as the light" (Matthew 17:2), whiter than any cleanser on Earth "can white them" (Mark 9:3). We position ourselves to hear the Lord when we dress in white baptismal or temple clothes and are purified, "having the image of God engraven upon [our] countenances" (Alma 5:19).

We hearken unto Him when we obey His commandments. As when Peter, James, and John were in awe, we likewise hear the Lord best as we esteem Him highly and wish to enshrine Him in our memory.

When the voice of the Father came out of the cloud, saying, **"This is my beloved Son, in whom I am well pleased; hear ye him" (Matthew 17:5)**, the Apostles heard Him in power, authority, and majesty and then remained silent (see Mark 9:6); they bowed down in humility and reverence (see Matthew 17:6). Jesus touched them, saying, "Arise, and be not afraid" (Matthew 17:7). This touch may have had something to do with the fulfillment of Jesus's promise to give Peter "the keys of the kingdom of heaven" (Matthew 16:19). Joseph Smith taught that at the Transfiguration, these Apostles received "the fullness of priesthood or the law of God" (Joseph Fielding Smith, comp., *Teachings of the Prophet Joseph Smith* [Salt Lake City: Deseret Book, 1979], 158).[1] We likewise Hear Him when we receive the fullness of priesthood blessings and when we operate within priesthood authority.

Jesus commanded the Apostles to keep silent about this sacred experience (see Matthew 17:9) until "the Son of man were risen from the dead" (Mark 9:9). Peter obeyed this commandment and held his tongue until after Jesus's Resurrection (see 2 Peter 1:16–17; Acts 2). We hear best when we think less about ourselves and strictly observe the Lord's commands.

---

1 See Andrew F. Ehat and Lyndon W. Cook, *The Words of Joseph Smith* (Provo: Religious Studies Center, 1980), 211, 246, 285 n8, 331. See also the comment of President Heber C. Kimball that Jesus had "inducted his Apostles into these [temple] ordinances" (*Journal of Discourses*, 10:241).

Christ Visits the Nephites by Minerva Teichert

Christus by Greg Newbold

Hearing Him as His Covenant People

As the people in Bountiful had gathered at their temple, hoping to receive further light and knowledge and "were also conversing about this Jesus Christ" (3 Nephi 11:2), they heard a voice. It was not harsh or loud. It was small. But "it did pierce them that did hear to the center" (3 Nephi 11:3), causing their hearts to burn. They heard the voice say, **"Behold my Beloved Son, in whom I am well pleased, in whom I have glorified my name—hear ye him"** **(3 Nephi 11:7).** This invitation was extended to all present. We, too, can Hear Him as a people.

The yearning you've felt for something better is a yearning to come unto Christ.

—PRESIDENT HENRY B. EYRING

These people listened intently to the resurrected Lord (see 3 Nephi 11–18), as families, concerned for each other, and as disciples, charged with important duties. Prepared to keep His commandments, they listened in harmony to avoid disputations. They received His promises to all those who mourn, all who hunger and thirst, all the pure in heart, all the peacemakers.

They heard Him as he rehearsed the sacred Sermon on the Mount, telling them to be the salt of the Earth and the light on a hill, to suppress anger, to be faithful spouses, to turn the other cheek, to pray for enemies, to give to the poor, and to pray for the Father's will to be done on Earth as it is in heaven (see 3 Nephi 11–14).[2] He taught them about the gathering of Israel and the building of Zion (3 Nephi 15–16). They heard Him as He healed their sick, blessed their children, and administered the sacrament (3 Nephi 17–18).

I especially love how the Christus echoes these three-fold invitations for all the world to Hear Him. Bertel Thorvaldsen, who was commissioned to sculpt the Christus in 1820, portrayed the resurrected Savior, showing the signs of the Crucifixion in his hands, feet, and side, arrayed in glorious white. His arms are extended. He stands on a pedestal on which is inscribed the invitation, *Kommer til mig*, "**Come unto Me**" (Matthew 11:28). And a lintel beam directly above the Christus reads, *Denne er min Søn den elskelige hører Ham*, Danish words proclaiming, "This is My Son the Beloved. Hear Him" (Mark 9:7).[3]

Knowing Jesus truly did come into this world and that all can, without a doubt, Hear Him has blessed my life immensely. I testify that He atoned for the personal sins of everyone in the world—that He overcame death and invites all to come unto Him. Through the sure word of my Heavenly Father, I know Jesus is the Christ and that He lovingly guides and directs the progress of our Father's great plan for salvation and exaltation for all who will hear and do His will.

2 See also John W. Welch, *Illuminating the Sermon at the Temple and Sermon on the Mount* (Provo: FARMS, 1999).
3 For a full discussion of these details, see my article, "The Christus in Context: A Photo Essay," *BYU Studies Quarterly,* 54 no. 2 (2015), 148–161, at https://byustudies.byu.edu/content/christus-context-photo-essay#footnote-004.

It is in stillness that we are able to hear the Savior's voice most clearly and perhaps the word we will hear most often is Love! It describes his life, his way of ministering, his teachings and his essence. It describes what we experience when we hear him and when we feel him near.

—GREG K. OLSEN

As I Have Loved You
by Greg K. Olsen

Every Sparrow Is Known by Katie Garner

Using Our Minds and Hearts

BY TYLER AND KIPLIN GRIFFIN

How can you know, really *know*, that something is true? Have you ever been convinced something was true only to discover later on it wasn't quite right? God has provided means to help us prevent that from happening when it comes to eternally important truths.

"I will tell you in your mind and in your heart, by the Holy Ghost" (D&C 8:2).

What are the most powerful words in that scripture for you? There is a small and simple word that usually gets skimmed over in that verse, but it is one of the most important. It is the word *and*. Something amazing happens when a person has *both* their mind *and* their heart engaged in the revelatory process. Our efforts to Hear Him will improve if we better understand the role our heart plays.

The most important truths we learn in this life are often introduced to us through things we see or hear, but those truths don't stop at the retina or eardrums; they sink much deeper into our minds and hearts. From Nephi's perspective, when an inspired person speaks, "the Holy Ghost carrieth [the message] *unto* the hearts of the children of men" (2 Nephi 33:1; italics added). Most of us would have preferred Nephi to say the Spirit would carry the message *into* our hearts.

Notice the difference between those two words. If you look at the first letters of each word, it comes down to *U* and *I*—or *y-o-u* and I.

Let's pretend I am a student in your class or am sitting in a sacrament meeting in which you are

Lord of Heaven and Earth, Just Before Jerusalem
by Lee Udall Bennion

I want Christ to be present in my life because of the person I am when I invite Him in and the way He makes me feel. I compare it to floating in a pool of warm water that is completely still. The water stretches off into the distance as far as I can see. It flows around me and I can feel it surrounding my whole being. I feel supported but not constrained. If something crashes down around me, the waters quickly become still again. I become more aware of how I treat others and how I should treat others. I believe in the words of Christ when he testifies that we will all be joint-heirs with Him, to inherit all that the Father has. We are all children of God who loves us and wants us to succeed in the goals He has given us! President Lorenzo Snow said "I believe that every man and woman who comes into this life and passes through it, that life will be a success in the end." It is because of Christ that this is true!

—HOWARD LYON

As we incline our hearts to our Heavenly Father and draw near to Him, we will feel Him draw near to us.

—ELDER DIETER F. UCHTDORF

Let Not Your Hearts Be Troubled by Howard Lyon

speaking or am growing up as a child in your family. If you do your job, you will deliver the right kind of information in the right way. *You* will have done your part, and the Holy Ghost will respond by carrying that message *Unto* my heart but not necessarily *into* my heart. For the message to sink deep *Into* my heart, *I* have to do my part as a learner.

Christ Blesses the Children
by Clark Kelley Price

So exactly how do we open our hearts so we can hear at this deeper level? Let's take a close look at the word *heart*.

Heart begins with the word *hear*. When we hear with our heart, we *feel* truth. We sense things as they really are. We perceive light. We just know.

Looking even closer, you will notice an *ear* right in the middle of your *heart*. That ear is safely enclosed; it is not on the surface. This means your heart has to be softened and open to hear.

Now look at the first two letters. *He* is the focus of the invitation to Hear Him—not the world, not mortals, not the person at the pulpit, not people sitting around you. As good and inspired as some of those sources might be, the best they can do is to help the message come *unto* your heart. Only the Savior and the Holy Spirit, along with your proper use of agency, can help that message sink deep *into* your heart.

Now look at the last three letters of the word *heart*. This process of learning to Hear Him is somewhat of an art form. Like learning a foreign language, proficiency and fluency come with dedicated and repeated practice over time. It gets easier the more you practice tuning your heart to Hear Him. The more you allow God to soften and open your heart, the more clearly that internal ear can hear.

You will get to the point where you will be able to hear the voice of God speaking to you, even if His voice is subtle and comes as a faint feeling or whisper amid a loud chorus of contradictory voices. At that point, not only will your mind grasp and understand eternal truths, but your heart will also hear and know. Instead of being fractured and pitted against each other, your heart *and* mind will become one, each acting as a second witness to the other as your confidence grows in your ability to hear and recognize the voice of the Lord speaking to *you*, guiding you on your personal quest.

As you move forward seeking to Hear Him, rely on more than what you experience through your five senses alone; include both your mind *and* your *heart* in that revelatory process!

This essay is modified from chapters in Hear Him: Listening to the Voice of God in Scriptures and in Our Lives, Taylor Halverson, Lisa Halverson, and Tyler Griffin (Line of Sight Publishing, 2020); used with permission.

Jesus the Christ by Michael D. Bedard

The Tall Ledges of Mountain Peaks

BY SUSAN
EASTON BLACK

There's the good and bad about being a working mother. One good for me was having a morning routine. My three sons knew the routine—get up at seven a.m., eat breakfast, brush teeth, grab backpacks, get a hug from Mom, and be off to school. It was simple and worked well week after week. But if everything were simple and ideal, I wouldn't have much of a story for *Hear Him*.

One day, two of my sons got into an argument while brushing their teeth. It was over nothing but not to them. The argument became heated. My oldest son, Brian, retaliated.

Prince of Peace by Natalie Crossley

He Is My Friend by Susie Bytheway

Consider The Lilies by Trena Ward

"I can't find my shoes," John said at breakfast. "Brian hid them."

I looked at Brian and said, "You're too big for this."

Now there were three of us in a heated discussion. When the shoes were finally produced and the boys stood at the door waiting for their hug and send-off to school, I hugged John goodbye and wished him a happy day. I did the same for Todd, who was innocent of any wrongdoing that day. When it came to Brian, I had no hug or happy goodbye for him. My sons rushed off to school, and I did the same.

I had less than an hour to prepare for my Book of Mormon class at Brigham Young University. It was not easy for me to teach the Book of Mormon, because angel Moroni didn't give Joseph Smith a teacher's supplement. What I knew of the Book of Mormon, the students knew too. Preparing a class filled with interesting insights took time and much thought. As I read chapters in Alma for the day's class, the chapters were just words on a page. I could feel no Spirit in the words. I couldn't remember why I had underlined a verse. Not every class of mine was stellar, but this one had the makings of a complete failure.

> *Your Savior, tears of love and compassion in His eyes, awaits your return. Even when you feel far away from God, He will see you; He will have compassion for you and run to embrace you.*
>
> —ELDER DIETER F. UCHTDORF

I kneeled down in my small office in the Joseph Smith Building and asked the Lord, "What's the matter? I can't feel anything. Everything I've studied for the lesson is gone from memory. I can't even remember why I was excited to teach these chapters." While praying, I saw in my mind the goodbye scene at my front door and my refusal to give Brian a hug and wish him a happy day.

I ran to the next office and asked a colleague to teach my class.

"Where are you going?" he asked.

"Someplace much more important."

I got in my car and drove to the Rock Canyon Elementary School in Provo. I went to each of my sons' classrooms and asked their teachers if they could come out to the hall.

In a hall whose walls were covered with children's art of varying quality and bulletin boards that should have been replaced years before, my sons asked, "What's the matter?"

"Nothing is the matter with you," I said. "It's your mom who has a problem."

In my life, I had learned how to maneuver the foothills of the gospel, like not using alcohol, smoking, or doing something that might prevent me from successfully answering questions asked in a temple recommend interview. Outwardly, I appeared to take few detours off the covenant path. But there was another side of me to consider. I had failed to climb the tall ledges of mountain peaks in gospel living. That's where forgiveness, patience, kindness, and most of the teachings of Jesus Christ are found. That's where we learn to Hear Him.

Guiding Light by Annie Henrie Nader

Christ by Madison Wardle

I apologized to my son Brian in front of his brothers and told him I loved him and should never have sent him off to school the way I did. We hugged.

I learned that day there is a great difference between knowledge and the heart. There is great value in knowledge—through knowledge and righteous living the mysteries of the gospel are known. But if I want to soar into the eternities with those who had reached the mountaintops of gospel living, I need to change my life to be more kind, loving, forgiving, and patient with those I love most. Have I succeeded?

On that day in a hallway in an elementary school, I knew something of soaring to the tallest ledges of mountain peaks. Future days were not as successful. But isn't that what life is all about? It is a process of falling and stumbling and getting back up to hear the words of the Master and soar to great heights.

When I think of hearing the Savior, I think of a personal conversation. I think of Him speaking words that are specific to my life and circumstance. I think of Him knowing the details of my struggles with perfect empathy.

It has been an incredible thing to have recently become a mother. It has opened up a whole new world of understanding the Savior—His love, patience, and sacrifice become all the more poignant and tender. It is stunning to Hear Him teaching His disciples to be calm in the midst of a storm, and to not be afraid in facing chaos and the unknown. Motherhood has brought similar experiences of facing the unknown. However, Christ tells His followers to be of good cheer, for He has overcome the world. To me the Savior's perfect understanding of sorrow along with the ultimate joy He experiences is so perfectly parallel with parenthood—with all its challenges and the resulting joy of seeing a new little life grow and develop.

—ANNIE HENRIE NADER

Sacred Trust by Gaylynn Ribeira

His Voice Will Whisper Peace

BY LLOYD D.
NEWELL

For the past thirty years, I have been responsible for preparing the Spoken Word portion of *Music and the Spoken Word*. This brief message must be inspirational, nondenominational, and universally applicable, and it should feel fresh and new every week. It's a privilege, but it's also a challenge that I take seriously.

When I was called and set apart for this Church calling, I was given promises and direction that continue to guide my efforts today. The Spoken Word is

Christ and Sparrow by Dave Malan

always on my mind. As I read and ponder, in my conversations with others, and throughout the normal activities of the day, I'm always asking, "What would make a good Spoken Word message?" I have been blessed to receive inspiration from above with answers to that question.

However, despite my efforts to be spiritually observant throughout the day, I've found that, very often, the inspiration comes at night. A thought or insight awakens me in the middle of the night—I remember something I've read or a story or experience; something my wife or children or someone else said or did comes to mind—and the idea for a Spoken Word is born.

Other, more personal, promptings come too. Often the Lord uses these midnight moments to plant a thought about the needs of one of our children or about something I need to

Lord of Lords, King of Kings by Rachel Williams

repent of, to change, to improve. These messages are different from mundane or random thoughts that jump around in the mind; they are clear whisperings from heaven.

A few times, I've reached for pen and paper and written the thought down. More often, I only *wished* I had. As Elder Richard G. Scott said, "Knowledge carefully recorded is knowledge available in time of need." Recording inspiration, he explained, "communicates to the Lord how you treasure it. That practice enhances the likelihood of your receiving further light" (Richard G. Scott, "Acquiring Spiritual Knowledge," *Ensign*, Nov. 1993.). I'm also thankful, however, for these words of encouragement from Elder Scott: "Have patience as you are perfecting your ability to be led by the Spirit. By careful practice, through the application of correct principles, and by being sensitive to the feelings that come, you will gain spiritual guidance" (Richard G. Scott, "Acquiring Spiritual Guidance," *Ensign*, Nov. 2009.).

Faith of a Mustard Seed by Jolynn Forman

In His Tender Care by Sandra Bangerter Rast

As I painted this painting, I had continual thoughts of the Savior and the comfort He gives us as He watches over us. We are His sheep. He loves us each beyond our own understanding. I have told my children throughout their lives they will never know how much I love them until they have children of their own. Do we have the same understanding of the great love the Savior has for each of us? The Savior knows our past and also things to come. I used prayer often during painting to be inspired and to help those who view it feel the love of the Savior. I felt a strong impression that as we listen and Hear Him, He will influence us for good. The shepherd girl carrying an injured lamb represents that the Savior works charity and miracles through His servants. I thought of the times in my life when loved ones have carried me through difficult times, often unbeknownst to them that they answered my prayers. I know as I feel and listen through the still, small voice, we are constantly, every minute and second of our lives, "In His Tender Care."

—SANDRA BANGERTER RAST

Sometimes I wish I could sleep through the night like other people can. But I also know this burden has become a blessing; it is one way the Lord enables me to Hear Him. I think I understand the feelings of the psalmist who wrote, "In the night his song shall be with me" (Psalms 42:8). I have found that song to be a song of peace amid turmoil, a song of comfort despite heartache, and above all, a song of love and tender watch care.

Of course, I'm not saying that every night is a transcendent and heavenly experience; usually, I just want to go back to sleep! But from time to time, in specific and personal ways, I have received counsel, guidance, insight, admonition, hope, and peace in the middle of the night. How grateful I am for these moments of stillness, these promptings from heaven, these whisperings of the Spirit.

I am deeply reassured, especially in these troubled times, to know that God watches over His children and wants to communicate with us. As the psalmist promised: "He that keepeth thee . . . shall neither slumber nor sleep. The Lord is thy keeper [Psalms 121:3–5].

Years ago, on one of my Spoken Word messages, I spoke of an elderly widow who was our dear friend. I asked her if she ever felt afraid since she lived alone.

Spiritual knowledge, properly recorded, is available in times of need. If what I record is what I am feeling in my heart, the thoughts that come to my mind by the power of the Holy Ghost, it is akin to writing on small plates, sacred writings, prophecies and revelations. . . . It is hearing Him.

—ELDER DAVID A. BEDNAR

Her reply demonstrated the faith and conviction she had developed through many years filled with ups and downs, joys and heartaches. She said she was unafraid, because she knew with all her heart that God loved her and was watching over her.

As I said in that Spoken Word, "No matter how dark the night, we can feel heaven's light. That doesn't mean bad things won't happen. Good people will still suffer, hearts will be broken, and anguish in one form or another comes to us all. But we can trust in the Lord's promises" (Lloyd Newell, "A Song in the Night," *Music and the Spoken Word*, Oct. 2, 2010).

I have always loved this quote from the great French writer Victor Hugo, who wrote in a letter to strengthen a friend: "Courage, then, and patience! Courage for the great sorrows of life, and patience for the small ones. And then when you have laboriously accomplished your daily task, go to sleep in peace. God is awake" (Letter to Savinien Lapointe, Mar. 1841, *The Letters of Victor Hugo*, ed. Paul Meurice [1898], 23).

In quiet moments, day or night or anytime, His voice will whisper inspiration, peace, comfort, and joy to our souls. We need only Hear Him.

Young Christ by Emily Carruth Fuller

If Any of You Lack Wisdom
by Linda Curley Christensen

Throughout my life, I've wondered when a thought is mine and when it has hailed from another source. One principle has emerged: agency must be exercised. By seeking or asking, knocking or searching, this essential element or requirement must be met.

It's helpful for me to remember that the Spirit will not condemn without instruction or ask me to break my covenants. I've kept spiritual experiences journaled so I can look back on them, although I find that when I hear instruction from heaven, it is unforgettable. Even still, I write about it, as it feels very sacred to me, and I've looked for patterns and even prayed to know what His voice sounds like.

In retrospect, I realize how often I have heard His voice in answer to my questions, concerns, and needs. Oftentimes, the answers I seek come through words that fill my mind with understanding. At times, the words I need to speak in answer to someone else's question are given in complete and well-formed sentences. For me, the common thread in hearing Him is this pattern: ask, and it will be answered. Whether by heaven, by circumstances, or by others, it will be addressed shortly. Elder David A. Bednar called these answers tender mercies, love notes from heaven (see "Tender Mercies from the Lord," *Ensign*, May 2005).

It gives me joy to see the pattern and truth I have learned manifested in the incredible answer to Joseph's humble asking. The remarkable, world-altering events of early spring 1820 give humanity a never-ending amount of information to ponder. Since art is all about "seeing," I may never tire of painting or pondering the topic of the First Vision. Certainly, this was the first vision for young Joseph but not the first or the last for humanity, or especially for you or me. The key is having a sincere desire and a question. After all, "If any of you lack wisdom, let him ask of God" (James 1:5). In asking, we open the door to truly Hear Him.

—LINDA CURLEY CHRISTENSEN

I testify that the tender mercies of the Lord are real and that they do not occur randomly or merely by coincidence. Often, the Lord's timing of His tender mercies helps us to both discern and acknowledge them.

—ELDER DAVID A. BEDNAR

Answers to Prayers

BY ROBERT L. MILLET

Jesus revealed a marvelous truth, a consummate insight, when he explained: "I am the vine, ye are the branches: He that abideth in me, and I in him, the same bringeth forth much fruit: for without me ye can do nothing" (John 15:5). Truly we are nothing without our Lord and Savior. We are nothing without our God and Father. We are at best, as King Benjamin observed, "unprofitable servants" (Mosiah 2:21; compare Luke 17:10). Save there had been a plan of redemption, an atoning sacrifice, a means of recovery and renewal, even "all our righteousnesses are as filthy rags" (Isaiah 64:6). Such revelations are in no way intended to discourage us, to create within us feelings of futility; rather, it is important that we live and move and have our being clothed in a mantle of humility.

We live in a constant state of dependence. And yet as we begin to "grow up unto the Lord" (Helaman 3:21), we sense that such a dependence is not a bad thing at all. In fact, it is quite a marvelous thing indeed, for through relying upon Christ completely, wholly (2 Nephi 31:19; Moroni 6:4), we come to draw upon his enabling and sustaining powers, and by this means our God transforms weakness into strength (2 Corinthians 12:9–10; Ether 12:27). "And inasmuch as you have humbled yourselves before me, the blessings of the kingdom are yours" (D&C 61:37). We pray, and God answers. We thereby learn, are reminded, are chastened, are comforted, are challenged, are strengthened, are inspired.

There is a whole host of ways in which our Heavenly Father and our Savior may choose to communicate with us and sustain us. One way is certainly through the workings of our minds, through our thoughts. The Prophet Joseph Smith explained that the spirit of revelation may take the form of "sudden strokes of ideas" flowing into us (Joseph Smith, *Teachings of the Prophet Joseph Smith*, selected by Joseph Fielding Smith, [Salt Lake City: Deseret Book, 1976], 151). Enos, son of Jacob, wrote that the voice of the Lord came into his mind, affirming that his sins had been forgiven (Enos 1:5). On many occasions I have pleaded with the Lord for direction in the preparation of a lesson or a sermon. Often I have been for a time unsure, unclear about the course I should pursue, only to sense, at a certain point in my preparation, that ideas in the form of

Found by Regan Reichert

The Gift by Rod Peterson

scriptural passages, prophetic or apostolic statements, and even overall organization have begun to flow into my mind. Similarly, it has been my experience scores of times to be speaking or teaching in a certain avenue, only to have a related idea, experience, or unusual insight make its way onto the stage of my mind. I have never been disappointed when I have responded positively and actively to such promptings, and I have come away from such experiences knowing more surely that God is God, that he knows His children and their individual needs far better than I, and that it is in my best interest as His servant to follow where He leads.

In many cases answers to our prayers come through promptings as we read and ponder on holy scripture. We may well read of Peter's and Paul's doings or sayings and find immediate application to our own lives. We may study where Nephi sought the revelations of heaven, inasmuch as he knew that God was no respecter of persons and would grant to him as He had to Lehi (1 Nephi

By Robert L. Millet | 56

Tangible Light by Sam Newton

10:17–19), and we thereby feel motivated and prompted to do the same. Or we may be reading along in a section of scripture only to find our minds caught away to serious contemplation on another matter and soon come to realize that this mental detour was planned and orchestrated by the Lord.

Eyes to See by Torgesen Murdock

Christ Sketch 2 by Mary Sauer

"What a glorious blessing!" Elder Robert D. Hales exulted. "For when we want to speak to God, we pray. And when we want Him to speak to us, we search the scriptures; for His words are spoken through His prophets. He will then teach us as we listen to the promptings of the Holy Spirit" (Robert D. Hales, "Holy Scriptures: The Power of God Unto Our Salvation," *Ensign*, Nov. 2006, 26–27).

At the convocation of the College of Education at Brigham Young University in the summer of 1992, one student shared with her fellow graduates and others present a touching story about an experience she had had with a young Native American boy. He had been labeled by previous teachers as incorrigible, which was, of course, a serious problem. She felt impelled to reach out to him and help. She knew the family situation was difficult and thought that if she visited his home she might find some clue for how to reach him. The visit stunned her. She found poverty, neglect, alcoholism, drug abuse—everything negative and destructive seemed to be present in that home. Her heart ached for the boy; his situation made her despondent. As she poured out her heart in prayer to the Lord, she found herself asking, "Have you forgotten this boy?"

They Brought Their Little Children by Kwani Povi Winder

The answer came, quietly and reassuringly: "No. That is why I sent you."

Very often the Almighty answers people's prayers—the prayers of the lonely, the downtrodden, the hungry, the bitter—through other people, through those sensitive souls who open themselves to inspiration and are willing to be inconvenienced—those who seek to follow and emulate the Savior.

This essay is modified from *Talking with God* by Robert L. Millet, 2010 © Deseret Book Company. Used with permission.

It is hearing the scriptures in a feeling—a feeling in my mind, a feeling in my heart. For me, the scriptures are key in receiving and recognizing those thoughts and feelings.

—ELDER DAVID A. BEDNAR

His Voice Is Such a Blessing

BY CLINT PULVER

For me, Hearing His voice has meant everything, because it directs me as to where I should go, what I should do, and where I need to be.

When I was young, I had a dream of going to flight school to become a professional pilot, and when I got older, I acted on the dream and became a pilot. One of the most defining moments in my life as an aviator was when I soloed for the first time. I actually flew an airplane by myself! I could barely drive, but I was flying an airplane! It seemed crazy to me.

When a pilot solos, their instructor hops out of the plane, and then the pilot takes off and does three landings and three takeoffs.

Every Knee Shall Bow
by J. Kirk Richards

I try to hear the Lord by listening to the people around me, and in particular the marginalized, the young, and the powerless. The King of Kings, before whom every knee shall bow, said "Inasmuch as ye do it unto one of the least of these my brethren, ye have done it unto me." Matthew 25:40.

—J. KIRK RICHARDS

Recognizing Jesus by Sam Day

My instructor wished me luck and said, "Don't mess up," then sent me on my way. I grabbed the handle, cranked the throttle, and took off down the runway. I was full of uncertainty, and I was nervous and anxious with the anticipation of flying an airplane by myself.

When a pilot goes wheels up when they take off from the runway, they really have two options: they're either going to land and live to see another day, or they're going to crash and burn, so the margin of error is really small.

I went around the turn in the traffic pattern for my first landing and was working through the checklist of everything I needed to do when I heard my instructor call in on the radio. I'll never forget how hearing his voice brought so much comfort. I knew in that moment that I wasn't really alone, even though I

Peace Be Unto You by Gregory Mortenson

was flying the airplane by myself. I had somebody guiding me, I had somebody watching me, and we created a connection through the frequency that allowed me to hear him and for him to give me the direction I needed to fly safely to complete the mission.

When we look at this mission, or this life, we have our Heavenly Father, we have a prophet, and we have instructors the Lord has given us to guide us

through. I've always heard the Lord in my mind and in my heart, and He is the great orchestrator. He can see what I don't always see. And in the times I have listened, I have gained a stronger perspective that has helped alter my reality and influence a better story in my life. Those blessed moments have allowed me to accomplish more, to be safe, and to have peace in this life. Those answers and their guidance have helped me to not fall into the pitfalls of sin or despair or stress or anxiety.

His voice has helped me understand that despite the hardship or the frustration or the stresses I feel, I'm never truly alone, and if I do my part to

As a pilot I have touched the skies. As a church member I have felt heaven's embrace.

—ELDER DIETER F. UCHTDORF

That Ye May Know
by Ben Sowards

Following the great natural disasters and destruction that struck the Americas at the time of the Crucifixion of Jesus Christ, there were three days of darkness so complete that not even a fire could be kindled. Piercing this darkness, the survivors heard the voice of Jesus Christ saying:

"O all ye that are spared because ye were more righteous than they, will ye not now return unto me, and repent of your sins, and be converted, that I may heal you?

"Yea, verily I say unto you, if ye will come unto me ye shall have eternal life. Behold, mine arm of mercy is extended towards you, and whosoever will come, him will I receive; and blessed are those who come unto me" (3 Nephi 9:13–14).

Those who heard Him, found his arms of mercy extended toward them. They felt the nail prints in His hands and feet. They felt the wound in His side. Like them, we can choose to Hear Him and access the blessings of the Atonement in our lives.

—BEN SOWARDS

dial into that frequency by reading my scriptures, making sure I'm praying, making sure I'm standing in holy places, taking time to be still where I can actually hear that connection, hear that revelation that comes to my heart and my mind, it has made all the difference.

I did successfully solo that day and lived to tell the tale, and a big part of my success was my instructor's voice. The same is true in my life with the voice of the Lord—my greatest successes happen when I Hear Him. His voice is such a blessing.

Where Are Those Thine Accusers? by Rose Datoc Dall

Where Are Those Thine Accusers?

BY ROSE DATOC
DALL

When I read the account of the woman taken in adultery in John 8:2–11, I became fixated on Christ's question to this woman after He dispersed a mob whose aim was to use her as an object to entrap the Savior. He, however, did not fall for the trap but instead caught the instigators in their guile. With the mob having faded impotently away, leaving the woman bewildered and wondering at her fate, the Savior asks, "Where are those thine accusers?"

This question, for some reason, hit me with such force in such an unexpected and personal way that I felt compelled to paint this scene. I had an epiphany at those words: Christ, and only Christ, in all His mercy, is our only judge. Our neighbors are not, nor are our peers, nor our persecutors, nor the mob. Therefore, I chose to focus the viewer's eye on the two figures in the foreground: Christ and the woman placed dead center, with everyone else fading into the background.

We can lift ourselves, and others as well, when we refuse to remain in the realm of negative thought and cultivate within our hearts an attitude of gratitude. If ingratitude be numbered among the serious sins, then gratitude takes its place among the noblest of virtues.

—PRESIDENT THOMAS S. MONSON

Having said that, the most stunning personal realization for me as I further pondered Christ's question was that I found myself to be my harshest judge, much like most other Latter-day Saint women I am around.

I had an experience many years ago, when I was a young mother suffering from what could have been the baby blues, or postpartum depression in hindsight, but not realizing it at the time. Overwhelmed and stressed, with three children under the age of five, I used to beat myself up over lack of patience. I'd try to do better only to fail yet again, and I seemed to dwell on this fact. To compound fatigue and stress, I felt it difficult to stay on top of the endless chores while juggling young ones. Therefore, in my mind, I was a failure who couldn't keep up. I didn't measure up when I compared myself to other mothers who seemed to have it all together. Moreover, I irrationally feared that others would think me a failed mother as well. It was a vicious downward spiral of continual self-berating.

Then I attended Relief Society Enrichment Night, as it was called at the time, and the speaker, Sister Kaye Smith, gave a life-changing lesson about accessing the Atonement as a parent. She talked about being kind and forgiving of oneself. She taught how the Savior longs to assist us in our trials as we rely on Him. Her words spoke to my soul, and everything clicked. I learned that belittling and berating does not come from the Savior but from the adversary. I realized then that I was allowing the adversary to drown out the Holy Ghost, which made it difficult to hear the Savior, whose words would have exuded love, peace, and encouragement.

As we suffer through our own greatest of challenges, remember there is light and hope even if we can't see it. Remember Christ in Gethsemane and most importantly His victory over it. Exemplify His divine perseverance by following this one powerful truth: never give up.

—ADAM ABRAM

Our Savior by Deborah Baker

His Atonement is so vast in its reach and yet so intimate in its effect that it defies comprehension. We must learn to appreciate it more and more and more.

—PRESIDENT GORDON B. HINCKLEY

Gethsemane by Adam Abram

My inability to understand how to fully access Christ's Atonement in my life became debilitating. But He knows our struggles and suffered for every infraction and sin. This lesson turned my life around completely as I learned to rely on Christ's Atonement, to repent without dwelling unnecessarily on my mistakes, and to pray often so I can better Hear Him. "**He that keepeth thee . . . shall neither slumber nor sleep. The Lord is thy keeper [Psalms 121:3–5].**

Christ by Lynde Mott

Most things we hear from heaven are ultimately felt in our hearts. And then hopefully that feeling trickles up into our minds, where it helps guide us to follow what we hear.

—PRESIDENT M. RUSSELL BALLARD

In short, the woman in this painting is not just the adulterous woman; she is anyone who has ever fallen short or sinned or found it hard to forgive themselves. This piece is an invitation to Hear Him, a testimony that His Atonement and forgiveness are ready for all. Moreover, if He will forgive and forget any sin though they be scarlet, so should we, especially our own.

Hope Is a Thing with Feathers by Carin Fausett

He Knows My Name

BY HANK SMITH

Two hundred years ago, the world changed with just one word—*Joseph*.

What did Joseph learn with that one word? That God knows *his* name. And because of Joseph's findings, we can conclude that if God knows Joseph's name, then *God knows my name*.

This message that the Lord knows us individually is repeated in every book of scripture and illustrated in countless examples of all types of people, from Apostles to everyday Saints.

Be Still by Jay Bryant Ward

First Vision of Joseph Smith by Trevor Southey

I Am He by David Koch

The Christ by Derek Westra

Christo by Esther Hi'ilani Candari

For example, Elder Bednar gave his first conference talk in 2005 called "The Tender Mercies of the Lord." In it, Elder Bednar described the previous general conference, when he had been called to be an Apostle. He talked about the rest hymn right before he stood to bear his testimony.

Elder Bednar said, "If . . . I had been invited to suggest an intermediate hymn for that particular session of the conference—a hymn that would have been both edifying and spiritually soothing for me and for the congregation before my first address in this Conference Center—I would have selected my favorite hymn, 'Redeemer of Israel.' Tears filled my eyes as I stood with you to sing that stirring hymn of the Restoration."

Now, to all of us watching, that song was . . . a song. But to Elder Bednar, it was a tender mercy of the Lord. I call it a one-by-one blessing.

What was the message to Elder Bednar? "David, I know you. I love you. I support you. We're going to be in this together for a long time. Get ready!"

Elder Bednar said, "The tender mercies are the very personal and individualized blessings . . . we receive because of and through the Lord Jesus Christ." Do you think he got that at that moment—comfort and reassurance?

He said, "I testify that the tender mercies of the Lord are real and that they do not occur randomly or merely by coincidence."

Do you see why we love the Lord? He is so good to us.

A few years ago, I heard this story about a young missionary from Utah: Parker Strong, a nineteen-year-old boy from Centerville, Utah, sat on a bench in West Africa. He said the bus system was overcrowded, and passengers had begun passing their goods around for others to hold. He had been handed a goat, and the goat was breathing in his face.

He turned to look out the window at the rain forest they were driving through, and he said, "In that moment, it hit me: I am in the middle of West Africa." Apparently, being in West Africa had been kind of adventurous. He'd been able to get his own water, and they didn't have electricity, and it was like camping. But then he said, "All of a sudden, the excitement began to wear off, and the reality of my new circumstances set in."

He was longing for the luxuries of home. And he began to have doubts that this was the place where he could even share the gospel the best. He said, "I think it's natural for missionaries to feel that way. Is this really where I'm supposed to be? Is this what I should be doing with my life?" As the thoughts lingered, he got off the bus and was sitting on a bench in a tiny fishing village when he looked up and saw a young boy walking by wearing a Junior Jazz basketball jersey.

He Will Dry All Tears by Heather Graham

He said he looked at it and was like, "Hey, that's the Jazz. That's my hometown team. That alone was so exciting because it was something I recognized from home. I was like, 'Wow, that really speaks to me. That's so cool. A little piece of my home in West Africa.'"

He asked the boy to come over and asked if he could look at the jersey. The boy took it off and handed it to him. As he held it in his lap, Elder Strong noticed the jersey had the number zero—the same number he had worn years ago as a member of the Junior Jazz. He flipped the jersey inside-out to see its reversible side. "Inside, I saw a signature. There in terrible handwriting, the handwriting of a ten-year-old, it said 'Parker B. Strong.'"

Jesus by Barbara S. Badger

"That's my name," he said. "It was an out-of-body experience. I was like, Is this real? Is this really happening? Am I dreaming? Is this really in my hands right in front of me?"

Somehow, after Elder Strong had given his jersey to his mother years before and she had donated it to Desert Industries, the Junior Jazz jersey had found its way to West Africa and back into his hands. He said, "I think it was there to tell me that I was loved and I was cared for and that my Heavenly Father was watching over me." He handed the jersey back to the confused boy, who took it and left.

Some people would say that was a coincidence. Right?

Elder Bednar might say, "The tender mercies of the Lord are real."

Elder Strong said, "My life is going to be directed how God wants it to be as long as I am willing to pay attention."

My hope and my prayer is that you will go to the Lord and ask Him if He knows you. Let Him show you that He knows you, that you are loved, and that he is watching over you—you can Hear Him.

Compassionate Christ
by Kendra Parrish Burton

Our present circumstances may not change, but through God's compassion, kindness, and love, we will all receive more than we deserve.

—ELDER DALE G. RENLUND

Painting a portrait of our Savior that would be universally meaningful and that would convey His ultimate compassion has been my desire for as long as I can remember. A friend of mine shared an idea from a story about Christ that I found especially touching and inspiring:

Jesus, as a grown man, sees His mother, Mary, sitting in a softly lit room. He kneels at her feet, looking up into her eyes as He once did when He was young. In essence, He tries to find the right words to say as His mind is reminiscent of the many experiences they have shared as mother and Son. He then tells her, "My time has come and is at hand." Mary questions what He means, to which He responds, "On the morrow, they come for me." Through her concerned expression, she reminds Him, "Oh, Jesus, you have the power to save yourself." Then, with the most tender feelings, considering the magnitude of His Atonement that is soon to commence, He says, "Mother, it is for this purpose that I have come into the world."

A realization washes over Mary, and she wonders if this could be the last time she will see Him alive. As tears fill her eyes, she reaches out one last time to stroke her Son's hair and to gaze upon Him as she once did when He was a child. His compassion toward His mother, as well as every soul in the world, radiates from His countenance as He willingly fulfills the purpose of His life.

While painting this piece, I thought of all the relatives and ancestors who have gone before me. I completed *Compassionate Christ* one month after my father passed away and several years after my nine-year-old twin daughter passed away. I like to believe these loved ones helped influence this painting of our Savior.

He is real. He lives. His eyes are full of understanding, and His arms are open wide to encircle and embrace us as we personally experience the love of a very caring and compassionate Christ, who asks us only to Hear Him.

—KENDRA PARRISH BURTON

A Testimony of Experience

BY JOHN BYTHEWAY

The Father's words to Joseph Smith in the Sacred Grove are an invitation to all of us: "Hear Him!" Some have actually heard His voice. Some of us Hear Him through our feelings. We Hear Him through our experiences. We Hear Him through evidences He reveals to us, and we Hear Him when we witness how the gospel makes sense.

Feelings

Some have puzzled over why they have never felt the "burning in the bosom" mentioned in D&C 9, concluding that they're somehow unworthy or incapable of feeling the Spirit. But perhaps the burning in the bosom can be anything from just a heartwarming story to an actual warmth within. And not everyone comes equipped with that type of spiritual receptor. President Dallin H. Oaks once commented: "I have heard adult members of the Church claim they do not have a testimony because they have never experienced a 'burning in the bosom' (D&C 9:8). If I thought this scriptural 'burning' only referred to caloric heat, I would have to say that I have never had a burning in the bosom either. . . . In this usage, it does not seem to refer to heat but rather to an intensity of feeling. For me, the witness of the Holy Ghost is an intense feeling of serenity or well-being" (*Church News*, 29 April 1989).

Other feelings are perhaps more common than the relatively rare burning feeling. Some have felt peace in the temple, love and comfort at a funeral, or a touch of eternity at a sealing. We may feel enlightened in Sunday School, excited

Restoration by Kelly Lane Pugh

and motivated at a Come, Follow Me class, or enlarged at general conference. Feelings are, without question, one way we Hear Him but not the only way.

Experiences

A few years ago, I researched general conference talks on the topic of "Testimony," and virtually every one I found mentioned these verses: "My doctrine

Talitha Cumi by Eva Koleva Timothy

is not mine, but his that sent me. If any man will do his will, he shall know of the doctrine, whether it be of God, or whether I speak of myself" (John 7:16–17).

Notice that Jesus didn't say, "Just listen, and you'll know because you'll have a *feeling* that what I say is true." No, Jesus taught that we must *do* in order to *know*. That is a testimony not of feelings but of experience. Experience is another way we Hear Him. "More people," Brigham Young taught, "have received testimonies on their feet than down on their knees praying for them" (*Improvement Era*, June 1935, 384). A testimony of experience is harder to

Mysterium Fidei by David Habben

Prince of Peace by Erin Meads

dismiss than a testimony of feelings. As the old saying goes, "A person with an experience is *never* at the mercy of someone with only an opinion."

Evidence

Jesus once healed a man who was born blind, sending the Pharisees into a tizzy. "Who did this to you?" they demanded, prepared to cast anyone out of the synagogue who confessed that Jesus was the Christ. First they asked the man who was healed, then they asked his parents, then they asked the man again. The Pharisees finally threw up their hands and labeled Jesus a sinner, to which the man with new vision answered, "Whether he be a sinner or no, I know not: one thing I know, that, whereas I was blind, now I see" (John 9:25). How can you argue with evidence like that? Elder Jeffrey R. Holland taught: "The fruit of living the gospel is evident in the lives of Latter-day Saints everywhere. As Peter and John said once to an ancient audience, I say today, 'We cannot but speak the things which we have seen and heard,' and what we have seen and heard is that 'a notable miracle hath been done' in the lives of millions of members of this Church. That cannot be denied" ("Lord, I Believe" *Ensign*, May 2013).

Trust in the Lord, and never underestimate the impact your testimony can have upon the lives of others as you bear it with the power of the Spirit. Doubt and fear are tools of Satan. The time has come for all of us to overcome any fear and boldly take every opportunity to share our testimonies of the gospel.

—PRESIDENT M. RUSSELL BALLARD

Living, walking, breathing testimonies of the fruits of gospel are all around us, in our wards, stakes, and neighborhoods, and Jesus assured, "Ye shall know them by their fruits" (Matthew 7:16).

Gratitude is a fruit of the gospel. Moroni's promise is that if we read, ponder, and pray, we can know (see Moroni 10:4). But Moroni's promise is preceded by this admonition: "Remember how merciful the Lord hath been unto the children of men, from the creation of Adam even down until the time that ye shall receive these things, and ponder it in your hearts" (Moroni 10:3). Pondering the Lord's dealings with His children should fill us with gratitude. *Gratitude precedes revelation* and prepares the way to Hear Him.

Logic

I am grateful that the gospel of Jesus Christ makes sense. A God who loves us will invite us to be the best we can be. That only makes sense. Imagine what the world would be like if everyone practiced "love thy neighbor as thyself" and "do unto others as you would have them do unto you." Imagine what a pleasant place the world would be if everyone kept other commandments, such as "thou shalt not steal" or "thou shalt not bear false witness." If you ever have a question about a commandment or standard, ask yourself, "*If everyone lived like this*, how would the world be different?" Living the gospel brings happiness and lightens our burdens. The gospel makes sense! None of us keeps the commandments perfectly, and thankfully, we worship a God who forgives and invites us to forgive as well, but pondering the fruits of the commandments and how all truths work together to create a whole that just makes logical sense is another way we can Hear Him. The gospel makes sense in a world that often doesn't.

I Believe in Christ by Cary Henrie

Create a F.E.E.L. Journal

As a bishop, I enjoyed asking my ward members, "What do you know for sure?" Then, one statement at a time, we would create a list together. Some lists grew into a pamphlet! Many of us have forgotten how much we really know and how many times and in how many ways we have heard Him throughout our lives. As I read their inspiring lists, mine grew longer as well. Make your own list, and as King Benjamin suggested, "have it always before your eyes" (Mosiah 1:5). Why? Because we tend to forget how often we have heard Him, and when we Hear Him, it is vital that we remember.

This essay is modified from *How Do I Know If I Know?* by John Bytheway, 2014 © Deseret Book Company. Used with permission.

Listen to My Words

BY ED J. PINEGAR

God the Father commanded us three times to hear His Beloved Son: on the Mount of Transfiguration, in His introduction in 3 Nephi 11 to the Saints on the American continent, and to the Prophet Joseph in the Sacred Grove.

God the Father wanted to make sure we would hear and hearken to His Beloved Son and receive Him and follow Him in word and deed. In His great wisdom, He commanded the prophets to record the words of Christ so we would have them continually before us. As in all things, God provided a way, and we must choose what we will do with the tools. To Hear Him, we must ponder these words carefully (see 2 Nephi 32:3, 33:10–11; Jacob 6:8; Moroni 7:38) and all Holy Writ, for the word has more power than anything else to change our lives (see Alma 31:5) because Christ is the Word of God (see John1:1, 14; Revelation 19:13). When we are spiritually in tune, the Holy Ghost can prompt us concerning things we should do or say (see 1 Nephi 4:6; D&C 100:5–8). And at regular scripture time or personal gospel study time, we should prepare ourselves to hear the Lord. We should not just "get through" our scripture study; we should have an appointment with the Lord to Hear Him.

The Risen Lord by Arnold Friberg

As you appropriately seek for and apply unto the spirit of revelation, I promise you will "walk in the light of the Lord." Sometimes the spirit of revelation will operate immediately and intensely, other times subtly and gradually, and often so delicately you may not even consciously recognize it. But regardless of the pattern whereby this blessing is received, the light it provides will illuminate and enlarge your soul, enlighten your understanding, and direct and protect you and your family.

—ELDER DAVID A. BEDNAR

When we covenant to take upon us Christ's name in baptism, our relationship with Him deepens, as He becomes the Father of our spiritual rebirth (see Mosiah 5:7) and hearing Him becomes a vital part of that bond, a very tender part as we cry out for help . . . and He comes to our aid. He speaks to our mind and heart (the spirit within all of us) by the power of the Holy Ghost, and we Hear Him in a very real and sacred way.

On one occasion, I had a lovely visit with a couple who was struggling. The Spirit of the Lord was abundant. Everyone wanted to do good. As they left, I was pondering in my heart the wonder of it all and thought, What more could I do to show my love to my Heavenly Father and my Savior Jesus Christ? The prompting came as I walked out onto our deck, looked into the heavens, and pleaded with the Lord to give me more commandments to keep. The prayer was very personal and tender; I wanted to show my love to my Heavenly Father. Immediately, I heard in my mind, "Ed, my son, have another child," and I felt confirming feelings in my heart.

The little boy inside me said, "Oh, Father, wilt thou tell my sweetheart?"

The night ended, and I knew what I must do to receive the Lord's help. The following day, I started fasting one day a week for the Lord's help in guiding my wife to know that we needed to have another child now! Pregnancies were so difficult and trying for her. I prayed for her to have the strength to endure.

Ye Are Not Forgotten by Jon McNaughton

After the third month of my fasting, my wife came to me and said, "Sweetheart, we need to have another child now!" The Lord had answered my prayers and had inspired my wife with the desire to grow our family. We were blessed with

Christ Walking with Children by Wilson J. Ong

another child and another! And it came about because I had heard as clear as if the Lord had been standing next to me, "Ed, my son, have another child."

On yet another occasion, I experienced a tender moment in trying to help one of my struggling children. I share it though it is sacred to me because I pray that those who read it will receive it in a spirit of love and compassion and find strength in it. After several years of fasting and praying and shedding tears for my son, I was getting weak, and my pleadings were more intense. This night, tears dropped from my cheeks after a long and pleading prayer. And finally, the voice of the Lord came to me and said, "Ed, my son, he is my son too."

Thy Faith by Judith Mehr

It has been said that the source of interesting pictures is life and that life is a function of experience, or in other words, your experience is your life, and the most influential experience for an artist and illustrator, as well as their audience, is visual.

On my mission to Germany, I was able to meet, teach, and baptize a young art history student who was studying at the Free University in Berlin. In Berlin's Dahlem Galerie, she introduced my companion and me to some remarkable paintings, including several religious paintings by the Dutch master Rembrandt Van Rijn. The color and value in some of those works became inspirational to me when, a few years later, I completed my first painting of Christ.

Illustrators are visual storytellers, the word illustration deriving from the Latin illustrare, which means "to illuminate or make bright." I believe good stories can bind us together and reveal our humanity. Great stories help us explore possibilities.

Historically, the Bible and other important books and manuscripts had their stories illuminated with letters, designs, and paintings. I am grateful for a mother who read worthy stories to me as a child, including the stories of Jesus, and for other family members who have shared their extraordinary stories verbally and in letters and journals. I am thankful for a grandmother who taught me about her love for the Savior through the paintings of Christ she hung on her bedroom walls and the stories she willingly shared about her family's conversion to the gospel of Jesus Christ in Denmark and their subsequent journeys and trials of faith.

I am thankful for the scriptures and for the lives of the prophets. These experiences, along with others, have given me a stronger sense of identity and have helped me truly Hear Him as I have attempted to communicate a spiritual narrative and content in my creative work.

—ROBERT T. BARRETT

The Lord had heard my prayer and had eased the burden, and I knew my son was in the Lord's hands. God gave me peace, and life went on, knowing that the Lord was nearby and all would eventually be okay.

Remember to Hear Him—prayer precedes revelation, faith precedes the miracle, meekness precedes a visitation of the Holy Spirit (see Moroni 8:26). As we seek to follow our Savior Jesus Christ and Hear Him, let these words from His lips sink deep into our very soul: "Learn of me, and listen to my words; walk in the meekness of my Spirit, and you shall have peace in me. I am Jesus Christ; I came by the will of the Father, and I do his will" (D&C 19:23–24).

Christ the Creator by Robert T. Barrett

At-One-Ment by Jennifer Paget

Silent Music

BY TONI
SORENSON

One of the things I love most about the therapeutic work I do is being present when broken families are made whole again. It's the best kind of magic imaginable. I'm thinking of a father and son who hadn't seen each other in seven long, painful years. When the boy was sixteen, he left home. Depending on who was telling the tale, he was either kicked out or he ran away.

Now the young man was mentally and emotionally scraped and bruised from torpedoing his way to rock bottom. This wasn't the first time he'd been in addiction treatment, and his father let me know he was finished paying, hoping, and trusting. "I can't risk him breaking his mother's heart again."

The father had been a bishop when the son had left home. Now he was serving as a stake president, and he wore his pride like a bull elk wears antlers. The man was expecting a fight.

Stiffly, he and his son exchanged looks. Their eyes locked. They sat as far away from each other as the room allowed.

The mother slipped up behind her husband, glimpsed her son, and went toward him. The son rose to greet her, but the father held her back with a touch of the elbow.

The son and father stared at the floor, but the mother couldn't rip her teary eyes away from the face of the son she hadn't seen in far, far too long.

The father spoke first. "I love you, but . . ." He used words like *disappointment*, *weak*, and *troublesome*.

The son fought back tears. He used words like *judgment*, *overbearing*, and *stubborn*.

Straight and Narrow Gate by Cliff Dunston

Tones escalated until they were on the verge of an argument.

The mother wiped her eyes and whispered, "I only wish God would pierce *both* your hearts."

"Let's give Him an opportunity to do just that," I said. "Everyone sit in silence until you Hear Him become the therapist."

Christ Portrait by Jordan O'Hare

Beweinung Christi
by Joseph Paul Vorst

Awkwardly, everyone fell quiet and shifted in their seats as the room was wrapped in silence.

Tick. Tock. Tick. Tock.

One minute. Three minutes. Eight minutes.

I prepared to break the unease at the ten-minute mark.

But then a miracle happened.

"I'm sorry," both the father and the son said in perfect unison.

They bolted out of their seats and embraced each other and didn't want to let go. The mother's sadness turned to joy.

Healing began when ears and hearts opened to *Hear Him*.

We think that prayer is made of words, but sometimes it's most powerful without them.

"Be still and know that I am God" (Psalms 46:10).

I believe that to be *still*, you have to stop, desist, rest, and settle into the moment.

Bait by Bruce Hixson Smith

Imagine what music would be without stillness, without daring gaps between. The notes would be unending, brash, indulgent sounds; it's the space between the notes that makes the notes beautiful. I call that "silent music."

A close look at the Savior's life teaches us how to use stillness, solitude, and silence to hear the voice of inspiration, truth, guidance, hope, and, above all . . . love.

When Jesus had to prepare for a major work, He separated Himself (see Luke 4:1–2). When He needed to recharge, He sought solitude (see Mark 6:30–32). When He had to heal from grief, He went away by Himself (see Matthew 14:1–13). Before making an important decision, Jesus spent a whole night in prayer alone (Luke 6:12–13.) In the final hours of His life, in the shadows of the Garden of Gethsemane, our Savior separated Himself from His disciples

so He could atone for mankind (see Luke 22:39–44). Time spent in solitude is not really time spent alone; it's time invested in the most important relationship you'll ever know—it's time spent with God.

As part of my therapeutic practice, I perform sound-bath vibrational healings. When it works, it's an inexplicable spiritual experience. The problem is that I need a silent space in which to work, and we live in a world where silence is hard to find. We're addicted to noise. In order to find peace in the process, we must discipline ourselves—we must seek the opportunity to "be still and know . . ."

The prophet Isaiah lived in a time when nature made the noises, not whining engines and squeaking breaks, not pounding music or honking horns or shouting people. It was for us he penned, **"In quietness and in confidence shall be your strength" (Isaiah 50:15).**

Not My Will, But Thine, Be Done
by Keith L. Bond

Risen by Michael Albrechtsen

When life gets loud and hectic, overwhelming, I pray that you will create a space just big enough for you and God. Let His voice be the silent music that heals your heart and makes your feet want to dance. May you seek to Hear Him because He alone has the words that can pierce your heart and set whatever is wrong in your life right again.

Savior by Sharon Butler

Christ Portrait Study by Casey Childs

Hearing the Voice of God Leads to Creation

BY TAYLOR
HALVERSON

According to the Old Testament, one of God's very first acts of creation was to speak. At the voice of God, creation emerged from watery chaos: "And God said, Let there be light: and there was light" (Genesis 1:3). The elements heard the voice of God and obeyed. Light burst forth throughout the universe. God spoke, and because the elements listened to His voice, order came to creation. And it was good: "And God saw the light, that it was good" (Genesis 1:4).

Are our lives ever disordered? Chaotic? Confused? Lacking light or purpose? The Creation story demonstrates that God comes to create order. He separates opposites, puts everything into its proper relationship, sets its bounds, and, by establishing order, brings creation. When we hear His voice, we can have the chaotic darkness of our lives banished to its appointed realm. We can see the light of God shining forth in darkness.

The Kingdom of Heaven by L. Aerin Collett

All nature seems to bespeak the works of God.

—PRESIDENT BOYD K. PACKER

Whether artists are aware of it or not, most, if not all, that we as artists know about color and design we learned from the Savior by observation of His "Art". His art being that which is found in nature.

Two Principles of Design that the Savior used extensively in creating both heaven and earth and all things therein is the mathematical equation referred to as the Golden Ratio and the pairing or juxtapositional use of Complementary Colors.

Some uses of these principles in the painting Truth Restored are: the placement of the Father, Son and Joseph Smith are precisely in the Golden Ratio. The three rings of light around the Father, Son and Dove (Holy Ghost) on the right are the primary colors. The neutral red fallen leaves complement the vivid green plants. The orange yellow sunlight is complemented by the blue violet shadows, etc.

I absolutely love seeing evidence of both of these principles spread throughout all of creation. In them I hear His voice—it is comforting and deeply reassuring. My testimony is that He lives and is the Creator of all things in heaven and earth, the Master Designer.

—LEON PARSON

Truth Restored by Leon Parson

We are part of God's created order. We can learn from observing His other creations that hearing and immediately obeying the voice of God leads to goodness. If we seek to taste goodness in our lives, we can when we obediently listen to God as He creates our beautiful forevers.

God is purposeful in creating. He has a plan in which He seeks to save His children. He put into place the Creation so we could have a stage for

Each One Is Numbered by Christopher Creek

experiencing His salvation. We wonder at the joy the elements must feel knowing that as they obey God, they help support the conditions for us to experience the plan of salvation.

The Bible records God's creative acts to prepare the world for His people. And the Bible records God's acts of patience and love as He sought to teach and save His chosen people, the Israelites. One of His most important commands to them was to Hear Him, which He reiterated before He brought them into the promised land.

Hear, O Israel!: The Ancient Israelite Article of Faith

God was ready to finally bring the younger generation of Israelites into the promised land after they'd wandered for many difficult years. However, He had

It takes conscious and consistent effort to fill our daily lives with His words,

His teachings, His truth.

—PRESIDENT RUSSELL M. NELSON

some additional covenantal instructions to share with them before they crossed over the River Jordan. God revealed through Moses the book of Deuteronomy, which literally means "second law" or "second telling of the law." The book of Deuteronomy summarizes, expands, and clarifies the covenantal promises and instructions first delivered to the Israelites at Mount Sinai (see Exodus 19–23).

One of the revelations God established in Deuteronomy is what we might call an ancient Israelite article of faith: "Hear, O Israel: The Lord our God is one Lord" (Deuteronomy 6:4).

Hearing is first. Hearing is the alpha. God's words are the omega. Where there is no listening, there is no hearing the voice of God; His words effectively do not exist for the spiritually deaf. Without first hearkening to God's command to hear, we cannot live the commandments He reveals. Without first hearing God, we cannot know of the promised joys He has prepared for the faithful Saints. Who can know of any of the revelations or words of God if they do not first hear?

So fundamental is this ancient Israelite article of faith throughout Israelite history and religion that even today, Jews will tack a small, inscribed container with a small scroll carefully tucked inside at the entrance of each door. The outward-facing inscription is a single Hebrew letter derived from the first letter of the Hebrew word for hearing. As Jews enter and exit doors—which are symbolic transitional places—they are constantly reminded that in all of their comings and goings they are first and foremost commanded to hear! This ancient article of faith is as true and necessary for us today as it was when God first revealed it millennia ago.

This essay is modified from chapters in *Hear Him: Listening to the Voice of God in Scriptures and in Our Lives*, Taylor Halverson, Lisa Halverson, and Tyler Griffin (Line of Sight Publishing, 2020). Used with permission.

For You by Glenda Gleave

The Power of Revelation

BY LAUREL C. DAY

Think for just a minute about all the communication issues that arise when you interact with people, even when you speak the same language. It's hard to get intonations and meanings and expressions right, so is it any wonder that we sometimes struggle to hear and understand the voice of the Lord communicating with us? Mortal to mortal can sometimes be challenging enough, so of course receiving personal revelation from the Lord could be a struggle.

Joseph and the Christ Child by Niki J. Covington

I try to live my life so I am worthy to receive the Spirit as I paint. I petition the Lord for His help, and sometimes, I find that when I look back and see the result, I know the Spirit has been there.

In my painting "Come Follow Me," the Savior is beckoning us to come follow Him on the covenant path, into the waters of baptism, and up to the tree of life and the mountain of the Lord.

I know that when we do this, we can truly Hear Him.

—DEL PARSON

We have to remember that we are not trying to communicate with an unknown God. We are striving to communicate with our Father. Because we are literal children of Heavenly Parents, we have within us the ability to talk to Him and the ability to hear His voice.

The process of personal revelation is different for everyone. We have great examples of this in the scriptures. Noah received very specific instructions about the measurements and structure of the ark God commanded him to build (see Genesis 6:14–16), while Nephi and his brothers, in their quest for the brass plates, received the command to obtain the plates but were not given any details about how. They consulted with each other and trusted in God, but it took them multiple attempts to achieve their goal. Why didn't God just make it clear the first time, like He did with Noah? We don't know why sometimes revelation is clear and sometimes pieces of the puzzle are left to us to figure out, but we can trust that the process can be clear even when the revelation is not.

So if your experience is that you don't think you receive revelation very often or that when you do receive it, you're not sure you know what God is trying to tell you, you're not alone. It's not easy work. Sheri Dew once told me it's like learning a foreign language, and too many of us don't give ourselves enough time to learn the language of the Spirit.

Come Follow Me by Del Parson

A good place to start learning how the Spirit communicates with us is by taking a journey of personal revelation about ourselves and an assurance that God is keenly aware of us. When we learn how completely He knows us, we begin to learn how He talks to us and how we Hear Him.

As I was studying the New Testament, a passage struck me that had never struck me before. In John 1:46–51, it says,

And Nathanael said unto him, Can there any good thing come out of Nazareth? Philip saith unto him, Come and see. Jesus saw Nathanael coming to him, and saith of him, Behold an Israelite indeed, in whom is no guile! Nathanael saith unto him, Whence knowest thou me? Jesus answered and said unto him, Before that Philip called thee, when thou wast under the fig tree, I saw thee. Nathanael answered and saith unto him, Rabbi, thou art the Son of God; thou art the King of Israel. Jesus answered and said unto him, Because I said unto thee, I saw thee under the fig tree, believest thou? thou shalt see greater things than these. And he saith unto him, Verily, verily, I say unto you, Hereafter ye shall see heaven open, and the angels of God ascending and descending upon the Son of man.

I love this for several reasons.

Nathanael asked Jesus how Jesus knew him, and Jesus said, "I saw you under the fig tree."

And because Jesus saw Nathanael while he was under the fig tree, it was all Nathanael needed to hear in order to know this truly was the Son of God.

Why?

What was it about Nathanael's being under the fig tree that was so incredible for Jesus to have noticed it?

I've thought about that a lot. There have been a few times in my life when I have been so alone or felt isolated—these have been private times. Sometimes painful. Sometimes holy. Sometimes holy in their painfulness. But they have been private enough that if anyone told me they knew about them, I would be astonished—it would make me think they had a special gift. There are simply things in my life no one could know.

No one except Deity.

And that must have been what this fig-tree experience was for Nathanael. If Jesus saw him under that fig tree, Jesus had to be God, or the Son of God.

Keeper by Chris Young

I testify to you that God has known you individually. . . He has loved you for a long, long time. He not only knows the names of all the stars; He knows your names and all your heartaches and your joys!

—ELDER NEAL A. MAXWELL

Brothers and sisters, I promise you in the name of the Lord that He will never abandon His Church and that He will never abandon any one of us.

—PRESIDENT M. RUSSELL BALLARD

Come Unto Me, Savior by Yongmee Park

At the Temple Gate by Emin Zulfugarov

I can recall one moment in particular in my life when I was "under a fig tree." No one—literally no one in my life—knew about it at the time. I remember where I was and where I was forced to my knees, calling out to my Savior to save me.

And I knew He knew I was there. He saw me under the fig tree. And I knew He was the Son of God.

He heard me, and I, in return, heard Him, and it deepened my connection with Him and my understanding of who I am to Him.

This is joy. This is security. This is love. This is the power of personal revelation in our lives.

I am grateful for a God who loves us enough to speak to us in ways that we can Hear Him.

This essay has been modified from "The Power of Personal Revelation" by Laurel Christensen Day, from the 2019 Time Out for Women, 2019 © Laurel Christensen Day.

A Path of Sanctification

BY ROBERT A. BOYD

"And he said, Go forth, and stand upon the mount before the Lord. And, behold, the Lord passed by, and a great and strong wind rent the mountains, and brake in pieces the rocks before the Lord; but the Lord was not in the wind: and after the wind an earthquake; but the Lord was not in the earthquake:

To the Rescue by Robert A. Boyd

And after the earthquake a fire; but the Lord was not in the fire: and after the fire a still small voice" (1 Kings 19:11–12).

One lesson I've learned from Elijah's experience with the Lord is that the Lord speaks to us in small and simple ways. If we are not listening, we may not

Time for the One by Michael S. Parker

Hear Him. Several days after being asked to write about the theme Hear Him, I took my wife to the emergency room. It was a place I would take her once or twice a year, whenever her autoimmune disorder would act up. This was the worst episode yet, and she was having difficulty breathing. In the emergency room, a young nurse practitioner asked Eleah what her symptoms were. She explained briefly her history and that doctors had given us many theories over the years. This particular nurse was a good listener, and in the end, he expressed his surprise that she had gone so long without a confirmed diagnosis ...

———

My own experience with hearing Him has been a witness that Heavenly Father loves each of us today as we are. But He expects us to become better tomorrow. As His children, we are each entitled to hear His voice. Our ability to Hear Him depends on us embarking on the path of discipleship, a path of sanctification.

The Humanity of Christ by A.D. Shaw

When I was a young photographer, it seemed so easy to feel inspiration and direction, especially when I was photographing temples. But as I had special experiences and my testimony grew, I found the Lord was also requiring more sacrifice and work from me for the inspiration to come. He was expecting me to become better—He required more effort on my part. I needed to let go of things that were not spiritual, spend more time in the temple, make sacrifices. I have realized the Lord was sanctifying me in the process of my hearing His voice and direction.

There have been many times when the inspiration has not come until the last moment. I've learned there are other times when we have to let go of our desires for things to work out as we hope they will and lay our trust on Him, knowing that everything will be okay. And the times when it seems we are not getting direction from Him, we may realize it is because the Lord wants us to learn and choose our path. When we do, we can trust that if our choice is wrong, He will let us know. He is always there in the background, ready to point us in the right direction if we take a wrong step.

Jesus by Larry Christensen

There is one area in which I know we can always Hear Him, and that is when we are in the service of others. I may have to work for the answers to my own problems, but when I focus on others, I'm surprised at how easily the promptings come. Whether it's as a ministering brother, a neighbor, or a Gospel Doctrine teacher, the Lord will plant His nuggets of inspiration in our minds.

In my line of work I have often stood in front of the perfect culmination of lighting and clouds at the temple, a perfect scene ready for someone to show up and click the shutter, and the Spirit has whispered to me that there is someone special to the Lord for whom I am taking this picture. To take that picture for one person, someone Heavenly Father is reaching out to—in that moment, I am humbled and overwhelmed as I've felt how much He loves this person.

I feel the embodiment of hearing Him is to mold our will to be the same as God's will. A number of prophets in the scriptures reached this point, and the Lord told them that anything they asked would be given. It wasn't a reward for being righteous; it was because they had become so in tune with the Lord that they would not ask for anything He would not bring about Himself.

I know of no experience more sweet or feelings more precious than to heed a prompting, only to discover that the Lord has answered another's prayer through you.

—PRESIDENT THOMAS S. MONSON

The promise of having every prayer answered is ours if we change our prayers from asking our desires to pleading for the Lord's desires.

———

Back in the emergency room, this young NP felt a prompting of what might be causing the autoimmune problems, and he ordered a CT Scan, even though everything on the X-rays looked fine. He was right to do so, and they found a tumor on my wife's thymus gland that has probably caused her autoimmune problems for many years. This young nurse was elated to have thought of this, but we immediately knew he was an instrument in the Lord's hands in answering our prayers. Through this nurse, we could Hear Him.

Light of the World by Randy Gunn

Reflections by Carol P. Harding

Trust and Hearing Him

BY CHRISTIE
GARDINER

After weeks of living in the midst of a global pandemic with a mostly normal demeanor, the anxiety of it all finally reached my eight-year-old son, and he would not be calmed. What I pieced together from the few words I could get out of him through sobs was that he'd heard me listening to a news report detailing mass casualties of the COVID-19 novel coronavirus. He was fine giving up baseball, friends, and swimming lessons but had just realized someone he loved could actually die. He was afraid. When nothing else worked, my husband, son,

He Is Aware by Rick Shorten

and I went to the trampoline to find answers. (Many of our family's problems have been solved lying on the trampoline, looking up at the clouds.) We curled up together. I put my hand on his chest and felt the hummingbird-like beat of his anxious heart.

"Breathe, son," I said and began modeling inhaling deeply through my nose and exhaling through my mouth. After a few minutes, his breaths began to mimic mine. "Close your eyes. Say a prayer in your heart. Ask Jesus to be with you."

True Disciples by Jared Barnes

There are times when we have to step into the darkness in faith, confident that God will place solid ground beneath our feet once we do. And so I accepted gladly, knowing that God would provide."

—ELDER DIETER F. UCHTDORF

A few more minutes passed. His breathing slowed more. I watched him shutting his eyes tightly and could sense the struggle of his little body, mind, and spirit as he searched for the Savior.

"If Jesus were here right now, what would He say?" I asked him.

He got very still, and what we call alligator tears rolled out of the corners of his eyes. The spirit settled over us.

"That He loves me," he whispered. "He says He loves me."

"Yes, son! That's Him. You heard Him. Now you have to trust it."

I knew it was a big ask. I thought doubt would creep in and my son might think he'd made up hearing Christ's voice or that the idea of hearing Jesus was just his own wishful thinking. I began mentally preparing a peptalk to help him trust the words he'd felt Christ say. It was a speech left unsaid as my little boy took a deep breath, shot up, and started jumping on the trampoline—back to his normal self. He had complete trust in the Savior and the personal revelation he had received. My little boy had found the love and peace needed to face his life's challenges.

The faith of babes, I thought. *No wonder we are counseled to become like little children.* Jesus says, "Whoso . . . cometh unto me as a little child, him will I receive, for of such is the kingdom of God" (3 Nephi 9:22).

I think I, too, would have been able to initially discern the Savior's voice as my son had; however, I fear I may have lacked the faith to continue to believe.

Light of the World by Scott Sumner

Too many times, I have justified and explained away the Savior's voice. I've unnecessarily walked alone, lacking faith and trust in my ability to commune with Him—especially in unconventional situations.

Do we trust ourselves when we Hear Him in unexpected places and at unexpected times? Do we trust the scriptures telling us to "ask and [we] shall receive"?[1] Yes, we Hear Him in the temple, in church, in the scriptures. But let us not limit the reach of our Savior. He meets us where we are and when we are ready to open our spiritual ears and trust what He says. Jesus speaks in ways He knows we will uniquely understand. I Hear Him in song lyrics, bluebirds, the orange-pink of a sunset, my children's laughter, yoga class, and, yes, even on trampolines. How do *you* Hear Him?

I believe each of us is capable of Hearing Him "better and more often," as President Nelson has counseled (see "President Nelson Invites Us to Hear the Voice of the Lord," February 26, 2020, www.youtube.com/watch?v=sGhQym_vhFU). He is with us, not only as a witness to our lives but also as an active participant in them. Our Savior Brother walked into a garden and became intimately acquainted with each human who has ever or will ever walk this earth. He felt the weight of not only our sin but also our sorrows, our fears, our failures, our triumphs, and our joys. He completely knows us and loves us in our totality. Being seen, accepted, and loved in whole—that is the gift of Gethsemane. He knows how to speak to us because He knows *us*. Each of us can Hear Him better and with increased awareness when we trust Gethsemane.

Life here on earth isn't always easy, but Jesus promised He would not leave us comfortless (see John 14:18). He promised us He would be on all sides (D&C 84:88). He promised He was the way, the truth and the life (John 14:6).

Put your hands on your heart. Breathe deeply. If Christ were with you right now, what would He say? Open your ears, trust your heart, and Hear Him.

What is said is not as important as what we hear and what we feel.
—ELDER ROBERT D. HALES

---

1 Too many scriptures to list contain some form of "ask and ye shall receive"—3 Nephi 27:28–29; John 16:23–24; D&C 88:63 . . . etc.

When I painted this image, I finished Christ's eyes first. Each morning when I came into my studio, these giant eyes seemed to pierce through me. On days when I was struggling or there were sad things going on in the world, I would look into His eyes and feel better. I often felt the words, "I am stronger than your storm, Heather." I thought about naming the painting "Stronger Than Your Storm," but in the end, I named it *It Is I* because one morning before painting, I was reading Matthew 14. The Apostles were in the midst of waves in the sea. When they saw Christ walking on water, they were afraid. The scriptures say, "But straightway Jesus spake unto them, saying, be of good cheer; it is I; be not afraid."

"It is I . . ."

To me He's saying, "I'm here. I know you, and you know Me. I love you, and it'll be okay." He's pleading with us to Hear Him. I find comfort in the way He spoke to them, like He knew them intimately and, in return, knows us the same. My prayer is that if anyone wonders if Christ cares for them, they can look into this painting's eyes and feel His undying love. He is direct. He can see our struggles, and He is not afraid. He asks only that we Hear Him.

—HEATHER FALTER

It Is I by Heather Falter

The Founders of This Great Nation Heard Him

BY STEPHEN R. CHRISTIANSEN

Though I have served for only a short-time as a member of the Utah House of Representatives, I have long been filled with a love of our nation. It likely began as I grew up in a home with a major general and patriot as a father. However, it was further strengthened in 1985 when I worked as an intern in Washington, D.C. for a former Utah Senator. Since those early years, I have been filled with a passion and admiration for our country and our Constitution. It has become exceedingly clear to me that many individuals who were part of critical hinge points in the history of this land were divinely guided. Indeed, when we speak of hearing Him, we must never ignore how those who established this great nation heard Him.

Christopher Columbus

Book of Mormon prophet Nephi beheld that "the Spirit of God . . . came down and wrought upon [a] man; and he went forth upon the many waters, even unto the seed of my brethren, who were in the promised land" (1 Nephi 13:12). Christopher Columbus recognized early and often the promptings of the Holy Spirit guiding his life. He said, "I could sense his hand upon me" (De Lamar Jensen, "Columbus and the Hand of God," Ensign, October 1992.). In addition to recognizing God's directing influence, Columbus acknowledged the gifts of the Spirit that blessed him to accomplish his foreordained purposes. He conceded that God "bestowed the arts of seamanship upon [him] in abundance" (Jensen, "Columbus and the Hand of God," 1992.). Columbus said he felt God's frequent promptings "to go forward" and said of His influence, "without ceasing [it] inflame[d] me with a sense of great urgency" (Jensen, "Columbus and the Hand of God," 1992.). It is clear to me that Columbus heard Him.

Come Unto Me by Glen S. Hopkinson

The Pilgrims

After a turbulent two-month ocean voyage, first aboard the Speedwell, then the Mayflower, the pilgrims sighted Cape Cod in November 1620. Among the group of 102 passengers, fifty Puritan separatists sought religious freedom to worship God as they pleased. One of the foremost among them, William Bradford, who later governed the Plymouth Colony, recognized the guiding influence of the Lord directing his own path. In his poem, Governor Bradford declared:

From my years young in days of youth,
God did make known to me his truth,
And call'd me from my native place
For to enjoy the means of grace.
In wilderness he did me guide,
And in strange lands for me provide.
In fears and wants, through weal and woe,
A pilgrim, passed I to and fro.

(William Bradford, "Providence and the Pilgrim," www.bartleby.com/400/poem/26.html.)

How grateful I am that William Bradford and the rest of those early settlers heard Him!

Serenity Prayer: Wisdom to Know the Difference
by Emmalee Powell

Founding Fathers

Without question, many of our early Founding Fathers who fought for and gained our freedom and established the constitutional framework of our nation testified of being led by divine Providence. Just two examples will suffice. George Washington proclaimed, "The man must be bad indeed who can look upon the events of the American Revolution without feeling the warmest gratitude towards the great Author of the Universe whose divine interposition was so frequently manifested in our behalf" (George Washington to Samuel Langdon, 28 September 1789, https://founders.archives.gov/documents/Washington/05-04-02-0070.). Benjamin Franklin, reflecting on "a transaction" (i.e., the passage and adoption of the U.S. Constitution) that came forth from

Lead Me Guide Me by Rex Price

a body of much diversity of opinion, acknowledged the indispensable hand of God in its creation when he said, "I can hardly conceive a transaction of such momentous importance to the welfare of millions now existing, and to exist in the posterity of a great nation, should be suffered to pass without being in some degree influenced, guided, and governed by that omnipotent, omnipresent, and beneficent Ruler" (Benjamin Franklin, The Life of Benjamin Franklin, [New York and Auburn: Miller, Orton & Mulligan, 1855], 322).

God Himself declared the importance of our Founding Fathers when He revealed to the Prophet Joseph Smith that our Constitution had been established "by the hands of wise men whom [the Lord] raised up unto this very purpose" (Doctrine and Covenants 101:80). Certainly, the Lord could not have "raised [them] up" had they not been men who heard Him.

Jesus the Christ by Judith Campion

God must be our North Star. He led our forefathers to this precious promised land. He preserved and protected this great land and fought the battles of the early colonists. He gave wisdom and inspiration to those who labored for four months crafting a document that would establish the most liberty-protecting government on earth. And He will continue to provide watchful care to us if we stay true to Him and commit to always Hear Him.

Deliverance Is Nigh by David McClellan

Oh, there is so much more that your Father in Heaven wants you to know. As Elder Neal A. Maxwell taught, "To those who have eyes to see and ears to hear, it is clear that the Father and the Son are giving away the secrets of the universe!

—PRESIDENT RUSSELL M. NELSON

In 2007, I was diagnosed with Stage 4 Chronic Lymphocitic Leukemia. At that time, I was self-employed in a family start-up venture that had long since wiped out savings and retirement, produced considerable debt, and, after eight years, was still trying to find its legs. As it was our sole source of income, every member of our little family worked full-time in the enterprise. Additionally, our attempts to care for aging grandparents were being seriously complicated by the Post Traumatic Stress Disorder (PTSD) of one grandparent and the mental and emotional illnesses of the other. In the midst of it, we were serving in a rewarding, but demanding, Church calling. Through it all, I found through lonely nights of pain and prayer that when voices of despair whisper that the Savior is not even searching for us in the rubble of our lives, those voices are eternally false. When they chant that He won't find us in time, or that even if He does, the best we can hope for is to gasp out the remainder of our days fit for nothing but misery, it's just not true!

Not long after the diagnosis, I painted *I Shall Be Whole,* my interpretation of the woman with the issue of blood (Matthew 9:20-21) in order to focus on the fact that Heaven has come down to us, and though we may have to stretch ourselves at times to what feels like our limits, the faith to touch the hem of His garment is sufficient to heal.

The Savior finds us in this fallen world because He literally loves each one of us, individually. He is the Savior because He never stops thinking of us, He never stops searching for us, He never stops reaching for us, He never stops planning for us, and never stops putting Himself in harm's way for each of us. His atonement is infinite, in part, because that's the only way to describe the lengths He is willing to go in our behalf. All our problems and all our joys lead to Him. In the first verses of the Book of Mormon Christ is referred to by the simplest title: One (1 Nephi 1:9.) I see in that the central truth that there really is only One answer, One solution, One way out, One way up—in time and in eternity. And that One is the One so named by the book of the angels, which brings us closer to Him than does any other book.

—AL R. YOUNG

I Shall Be Whole by Al R. Young

Woman at the Well by Crystal Close

Just Keep Taking One More Step

BY GANEL-LYN CONDIE

Waking up Monday, I sensed almost instantly that it was going to be one of those dark days where I would need to claw through every minute of the day, each tick-tock of the clock, until bedtime. I don't battle chronic depression and anxiety like my sister Meg did, but I do dance regularly with such feelings.

Mortality is designed to include moments of joy interwoven with periods of intense heartache. But for those who, as Elder Jeffrey R. Holland describes, "a dark night of the mind and spirit . . . [is] more than mere discouragement," no further description of *dark Mondays* is needed.[1] Fighting the *daily dance of the dark night* can make it more challenging and critical than ever to Hear Him.

I want to speak to those who fear heaven is open for business to everyone but them.

1 "Like a Broken Vessel," *Ensign*, November 2013.

The Lord loves effort, and effort brings rewards. We keep practicing. We are always progressing as long as we are striving to follow the Lord.

—SISTER JOY D. JONES

My recent dark day reminded me that when the fog of the soul settles into the crevices of the mind, it is then that I must pull out my spiritual toolbox and make every effort to just take the next step to Hear Him. Paradoxically, it is on the toughest days—when hearing Him is crucial but may be more challenging than ever—that depression or anxiety can stop our spiritual ears from hearing promptings, direction, or comfort.

As we wrestle to Hear Him, questions of faith, ability, and worthiness can start to creep in. The adversary plays with these doubts, convincing us that we are cut off from heaven—not capable or worthy of real communion.

So how do we Hear Him when anxiety or depression threaten to drown out all communication?

I want to share some steps I take to Hear Him, even when my soul screams, "Just stop! You are alone. You aren't worth it." I hope they will help you in the same circumstances.

I like to call the first step my *chopping wood and carrying water* efforts. I keep doing the things that put me in the place to Hear Him. Especially when I don't feel like it. I pray, even when it feels like a one-sided conversation. When my prayers feel too jumbled, I often write them out like a letter to my Father: "Dear Heavenly Father, I am really struggling right now . . ." And sometimes in the writing, I Hear Him.

I try reading the scriptures, even if all I manage is a single verse a day. Sometimes I rewrite a verse to include my name, something that helps me liken the scriptures to myself and, in the process, Hear Him.

All for You by Deborah Finneran

Forever in My Heart by Laila Flatebo Garza

At day's end, I record in a journal one way I have seen God's hand. Sometimes it is as simple as the sunshine or a hug from one of my children. Miraculously, I have never ended a day, even the darkest ones, without seeing at least one small handprint from God.

These basic steps create an anchor for my spiritual soul, especially when my emotions are being battered in the storm. I Hear Him when I talk with Him, read His messages to me in the scriptures, and focus on even one good thing in my day.

Second, I *call a faith friend* to help break through the fog of discouragement. My friend may not have solutions to my problems, but I know I am not alone, and that helps me Hear Him more clearly. Make no mistake, the adversary tries to convince us to isolate and to not bother anyone with our issues. But remember, he is a liar—so pick up your phone. A friend has often shared

Noble Parents by Elizabeth J. Stanley

impressions or insights with me that I later realize God was trying to send me all along. Receiving these loving messages from others has been truly lifesaving and has helped turn me toward Him. I Hear Him when I talk with trusted faith friends.

Next, *asking for and receiving priesthood blessings* opens my heart to Hear Him. I am blessed to live with a worthy Melchizedek priesthood holder, but I often wait too long to ask for a blessing. Life doesn't have to be horrible to ask for help from heaven. A blessing often makes a burden lighter, even if it's His will for us to continue carrying that burden. Blessings have often impressed me with new ideas, inspired me to try one more thing, strengthened me to take one more step of faith. I Hear Him when I receive priesthood blessings.

Finally, I simply *listen to uplifting music*. If you come to my home, regardless of the time of day, you will likely hear inspiring music playing. When the dark threatens to overtake me and when I become weary and discouraged, I turn up the light by turning up the music. I Hear Him in music.

These steps of faith are relational, not transactional. I am learning, and I am finding strength to keep trying, even when the steps I take feel like they are leading nowhere.

Jesus Christ by Haley Miller

God loves our trying. I invite you to just keep stepping forward in faith, even into the dark, to Hear Him and the words of comfort He has just for you.

In so many ways, all of us are like children. We are fearful, weak, and quick to forget why we're here. We fall and bruise ourselves and don't truly get back up until our Savior picks us up. We trip and stumble until we realize our Redeemer can carry us. Will life always be easy in the Lord's care? Absolutely not. We are not here to vacation but to be tried, stretched, and grown.

We followed our Chosen Leader into mortality because through Him, we can become like our Father. And we follow Him now for happiness, healing, and blessings. His light will forever chase our darkness away because as we daily strive to be more like Him, His light can become ours until it brightens all aspects of our lives and illuminates the way forward! In exchange for this light, He asks only that we Hear Him, that we follow Him with full purpose of heart. What amazing blessings from the Savior of the World!

—DAN WILSON

Healing and Rest by Dan Wilson

Jesus el Cristo by Jorge Cocco Santángelo

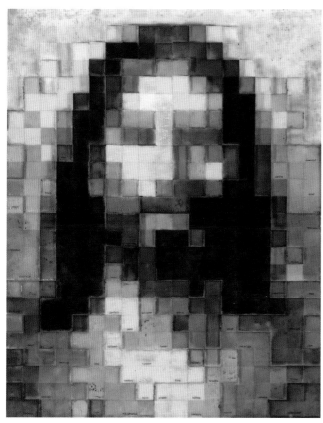

Hear Him by Megan Welker

Mio Cristo by Shari Lyon

To Treasure the Master's Words

BY JORGE COCCO
SANTÁNGELO

The command to Hear Him, in my opinion, goes much further than the simple physical function of listening to a voice with our ears. When the Father affirms this command, He uses it as a metaphor, indicating that we must live according to the Savior's guidance.

Throughout sacred history, many heard the voice of Lord, but few understood what He said. To mention just two events that exemplify the state of our sensitivity to the spiritual voice, we see that in John 12, the Greeks and others heard only thunder in response to the Lord's prayer or thought it was the voice of an angel. Only a few understood God's message.

The other event occurred after the enormous telluric cataclysms prior to the Lord's arrival on the American continent (see 3 Nephi 11). The first and second times God spoke to them, the multitude heard a voice that pierced them to the center, but they did not understand it. It was necessary for them to look attentively toward heaven to finally understand the meaning the third time they heard the voice.

Our loving Heavenly Father has not given us every answer.
He expects us to figure out many things for ourselves. He
expects us to believe—even when it's difficult to do so.
—ELDER DIETER F. UCHTDORF

However, I believe that up to this point, people still had to open their hearts to treasure the Master's words enough to put them into practice.

In both cases, the people who had made the previous effort to be prepared had developed more sensibility to hear and understand the voice of God; those are the true disciples of Christ, who are willing to follow and obey Him.

In addition to listening strictly in regard to our obedience to the commandments, the directive to open our hearts to the voice of the Lord and truly Hear Him and act extends to our earthly mission and purposes.

Personally, I can assure you, and this according to the promise that has been given to us, that through the Spirit, His voice may be emitted often and in abundance. We can benefit from it, but many times, we do not pay attention to such feelings. We must learn to desire these moments and act on them. As we do, they will become easier to hear and understand because the Lord's messages often come to our minds in a perfectly understandable form, in our spoken language.

As a visual artist, I can affirm that many of the themes I paint are presented or suggested to me in the form of images I can later record in a quick sketch. Obviously, next comes an arduous intellectual effort and the exercise of using all my training and practice in the arts.

The Road to Jerusalem by Michael Coleman

According to these experiences, I believe the light of Christ illuminates every being according to their vocation, office, or function that has been assigned to them as a gift to develop in this life. This same principle of inspiration in professional development applies in all areas of our life, including our personal and family development. Therefore, it will be our duty to refine our perception of that wonderful voice that speaks to us to better fulfill our purpose among our fellow men. Then, Hear Him!

On the Way to the Other Side by Colby A. Sanford

His Hands by Greg Sargent

Light of Life by Melissa Tshikamba

In order to enjoy the refuge that Jesus Christ and His Atonement offer, we must have faith in Him—a faith that will allow us to rise above all the pains of a limited, earthly perspective. He has promised that He will make our burdens light if we come unto Him in all that we do.

—ELDER RICARDO P. GIMENEZ

Raising the Daughter of Jairus by Jeremy Winborg

He Lifts Me by Sabina Morrey

Jesus the Christ by Brendan Clary

If I May but Touch

BY GLENN
RAWSON

It began on the beach at Capernaum. As Jesus came ashore, the people were waiting (see Luke 8:40). Among them was Jairus, a ruler of the synagogue who fell at His feet and announced that his only daughter lay dying. "I pray thee, come and lay thy hands on her, that she may be healed; and she shall live" (Mark 5:22). Thronged by a crowd anxious to see the miracle, Jesus began to follow Jairus up the street into the city. Within that crowd was a woman afflicted with an incurable disease—some manner of blood disorder (see Luke 8:43). For twelve years she had suffered many things at the hands of many physicians and was not healed but was more sickly than ever (see Mark 5:26).

Somehow, we do not know when or where, she learned of the power of the Great Healer. Faith was awakened within her, and she determined to go to Him. However, because of the nature of her illness, she was unclean under the Mosaic law and was ashamed to ask for the Savior's help.

For me, all things can and do testify of Christ. Every time I do a painting, I try to create that feeling in the painting. I love to create a visual impression that will reach out to our spiritual nature; especially if it is virtuous, lovely, or a good report or praiseworthy. Like Paul, I wish for all to think on these things (see Philippians 4:8); this can stimulate the mind to deeper reflection. So I like to choose subjects and techniques that are impressionistic. This painting of Christ "Among His Sheep" speaks volumes to my soul and among all the sheep I can hear His voice speaking to me.

—JULIE ROGERS

Among His Sheep by Julie Rogers

As Jesus passed by in the crowd, she said to herself, "If I may but touch [the hem of] his garment, I shall be whole" (Matthew 9:1).

It must have taken considerable effort and faith, especially for a weak and sickly woman, to even reach Jesus because of the crowd thronging and pressing Him (see Luke 8:45). Moreover, the distance from the lake's shore to the city

I find great hope in the assurance that no one is ever lost to the Lord—no matter our circumstances, no matter how alone we may feel.

—ELDER GERRIT W. GONG

was not far. The woman had no time to dally or waste with indecision. She pushed her way through and, from behind, touched the hem of the Master's robe. Immediately, there was a tangible surge of power that flowed throughout her body (see Luke 8:44). She was fully healed from that very moment and knew it (see Mark 5:29)!

Jesus stopped and said, "Who touched my clothes?" (Mark 5:30).

In effect, Peter said to Him, "All these people are pushing and shoving, and you ask, 'Who touched me?'" (see Luke 8:45).

But her touch was different from all the others'. Hers was a touch of faith and supplication that brought forth His divine power, and He felt it. "I perceive," He said, "that virtue [power] is gone out of me" (Luke 8:46).

The woman, knowing that she was discovered, came forward and fell at His feet, confessing before all what she had done. With intimate kindness and tenderness, He commended her: "Daughter . . . thy faith hath made thee whole; go in peace" (Luke 8:48).

How like that woman are we? In our time, President Russell M. Nelson has invited us to Hear Him and then added,

> As we seek to be disciples of Jesus Christ, our efforts to hear Him need to be ever more intentional. It takes conscious and consistent effort to fill our daily lives with His words, His teachings, His truths.
>
> We simply cannot rely upon information we bump into on social media.

(President Russell M. Nelson, "Hear Him," *Ensign*, May 2020)

Touch of Faith by R. Weston Lamplugh

We are like that woman, mostly nameless and faceless in a very large world, yet to Jesus Christ, we matter, and He has time and love enough for us. Like her, we all have hidden ailments that come with mortality and steal from us our happiness, peace, and power—ailments that the wisdom of the world cannot heal.

However, whether or not we put forth the intentional effort to "draw near" (Doctrine and Covenants 88:63) unto Him is our choice. It is for us as it was

Prince of Peace by Lynne Millman-Weidinger

Prince of Peace took more than five years to complete. It came about after my friend challenged me to paint the Savior, though I wasn't ready at the time. In fact, it was fifteen years later when I felt a prompting to start this painting and that I should not use a model. Following the Spirit and with the help of my friend, I began.

Almost immediately, problems arose within my family. My environment wasn't spiritual, and with the adversary working hard on us, I wondered how I could do such a sacred painting.

Before the painting was completed, I ended up in the hospital, recovering from an emergency operation. I was in the hospital for four weeks. While there, I had my own personal witness of the Lord when I felt His hands hold my face as He looked into my eyes. That feeling of love was encompassing, and I could not hold back my tears of joy. The Spirit was so strong that I knew then that my life in mortality was not over. I needed to be here for my family, and I needed to complete this painting.

As hard as it was to be in the hospital, it was nothing compared to what came after. I went through the hardest time of my life, my own personal Gethsemane. I learned firsthand what it was to have heartache and pain. I was being taught lessons that would bring me closer to Him. This painting isn't so much about Christ's physical appearance as it is the emotion of what He felt and went through for all of us. Over a long period of time, I overcame fear and replaced it with faith, turning everything over to the Lord—I learned to let go and let God. I learned to listen to Him and trust that He knows everything from the beginning to the end.

Finally, after what seemed like an eternity to me, I finished the painting. I had learned many lessons, and I was a stronger person for it. Creating *Prince of Peace* was a life-changing experience filled with miracles and trials. I pray this painting will bring comfort to all who see it and that it will help everyone in good times as well as in our darkest hours.

—LYNNE MILLMAN-WEIDINGER

for the woman healed from her issue of blood—with the presence of social media, it is as though there is a loud and pushing crowd about us, demanding with an incessant cacophony our constant attention. Will we tune them out and with single-minded determination fight our way to the Savior's side, where we can Hear Him and receive His power and peace?

The woman's enduring and endearing proof of faith was that she fought her way into His presence and touched Him with "real intent" (Moroni 7:9) and "full purpose of heart" (D&C 17:1). May it be so with us.

Watch with Me by Jeff Ward

Christ Healing the Daughter of Jairus by Lester Yocum

Hearing His Voice for the First Time

BY ALYSSA
EDWARDS

I grew up hearing incredible stories of people hearing the voice of God. Whether it was experiences shared during fast and testimony meeting at the start of the month, the grandiose stories scattered through the scriptures, or the examples shared during general conference, I felt like everyone around me heard God, except me. Little did I know, I was simply not aware of how to Hear Him.

I remember Hearing Him for the first time in 2014, or at least, I thought that was the first time I had heard Him. I was a missionary in the Guatemala City East Mission and had just woken up from a surgery—sounds like the start to a poorly executed joke, but it was my reality. I was sick during much of my mission, which ultimately led me to that post-operation room, the nicest room I had seen in months (other than the bloodstained sheets). It was a dark room with a small fan that blew on me every six seconds, and my sweet mission companion was fast asleep on a makeshift bed on the floor. Despite my companion's presence in the room, I felt completely alone. I was absolutely afraid.

I sat in that bed weeping and unable to move my lower extremities. I cried
out to my God and asked why. The tears continued to run down my cheeks
as I attempted bargaining with God, and then I heard a physical voice that
certainly did not belong to my companion or me. I listened to the instructions,
reached over to my backpack, and pulled out a small notebook I had filled prior

My Redeemer Lives
by Roger Loveless

I chose to portray the sacred events of that first Easter from the perspective of Mary Magdalene.

Upon returning to the tomb that glorious morning, the sorrowing Mary still not comprehending that Christ had risen from the dead, looked inside to find His body gone and assumed it had been stolen. In her sorrow she turned from the tomb, now having lost her last connection with the Lord and retired to a rock with handkerchief in hand to mourn His loss.

When Christ appeared and asked her why she was weeping, she thought he was the caretaker and said, "They have taken away my Lord." Jesus then said, "Mary," and she immediately recognized His voice.

At that moment, Mary released her complete and total sorrow, which is represented by the falling handkerchief and reached out with joy and hope to the resurrected Lord. "My Redeemer Lives" reflects the extraordinary moments of that morning, as seen through the eyes of one person, but will someday be experienced by all.

—ROGER LOVELESS

to leaving for Guatemala. I flipped open the little spiral-bound pad to a page where I had recorded a single verse from the Doctrine and Covenants: "The son of man hath descended below all things, art thou greater than He?" (D&C 122:8).

The tears cascaded down my cheeks now as I sobbed. I had not been abandoned. I was not the first to be deeply afraid, I was not the first to be utterly alone, I was not the first to question my God, and I was not going to be the last. The Savior descended below all things, including operations in Guatemala. This moment was pivotal in my understanding of the Atonement and also in my understanding of how I hear my Savior.

I have counted that moment as the first time I actually heard Him, but there is no way that is correct. I do not believe a God of miracles would wait until I was twenty years old to talk with me. It is clear I heard Him prior to that. I heard

Our Father knows that when we are surrounded by uncertainty and fear, what will help us the very most is to hear His Son. Because when we seek to hear—truly hear—His Son, we will be guided to know what to do in any circumstance.

—PRESIDENT RUSSELL M. NELSON

him when I was six years old, when my aunt returned from her mission, and I knew I needed to go on one. I heard Him when I felt the prompting to record the reference from the Doctrine and Covenants. I heard Him when I followed the impression to pack that small notebook in my backpack prior to leaving on my mission. Hearing is so much more than the physical act of listening to sounds and turning them into words. Hearing Him is knowing Him, is feeling Him, is understanding Him.

So how do we Hear Him? I am sure my parents, my leaders, and my teachers taught me about hearing the Savior, but I could not grasp the concept until I experienced it myself. I went years and years believing the Savior was not communicating with me and that there had to be something wrong with me, but that is just not true. I am so grateful that despite my not realizing He was speaking to me, Jesus kept speaking and continually reaching out to me. How patient of Him to speak when I was not understanding or acknowledging that Deity was actually communicating with me.

The moment I realized the Savior speaks in more ways than just words, I became quicker to recognize my own thoughts and feelings as impressions from Him. I know that if He is speaking to me, He is most certainly speaking to you! It seems as though the most important thing for us to realize is that the way in which He communicates with us is so very personal, and the way I Hear Him will be different from the way you Hear Him, and that is beautiful. If you feel as though you cannot Hear Him, pay attention to your thoughts, feelings, and impressions because I guarantee He is speaking—all we need to do is figure out how we Hear Him.

His Image in My Countenance by Sheri Lynn Boyer Doty

This beautiful green pasture reminds me of the countryside I loved to roam as a boy growing up in England. The path in this painting represents our journey through life, and Christ is on the path watching over us. He is the Savior of all who will accept Him, but most importantly He is the Savior for us individually. In this painting the Savior is caring for the individual lamb while also watching over the entire flock. The healing, comfort, and peace that only He can offer is a gift that is given individually in our lives. More than anything in this image I want people to feel the love and peace that comes from knowing that our Savior is there, watching over us.

—SIMON DEWEY

Dear to the Heart of the Shepherd by Simon Dewey

Beside Still Waters

BY BRENT L. TOP

C. S. Lewis insightfully observed, "God wants to give us something, but cannot because our hands are full—there's nowhere for Him to put it" (*The Problem of Pain*, 96). If I could amplify and update Lewis's words, I would say, "God wants to say something vitally important to us, but we can't hear Him—because the kids are screaming, we're on the phone, we're connected to several devices, we have ADHD, or all of the above."

Lilies of the Field by Cortney Lunt

We live in a world with all kinds of noise—external and internal. Our busy lives, our high-tech "toys" (some prefer to call them "tools"), and the ubiquitous background noise of modern society are but a few examples of the external noise that prevent us from hearing the Lord and learning what He would have us know, do, and feel.

In addition, internal noise comes in the form of all kinds of worries and woes that rattle around in our heads, creating such an emotional clatter that we can neither Hear Him nor comprehend His mind and will for us. When I desire to hear His voice, feel His Spirit, and learn of Him—especially when I am discouraged, depressed, or desperately in need of strength—I have to make extra time and exert extra effort to meditate. I am not necessarily talking about yoga meditation, hypnotic concentration, or visualization exercises, though each of these may be helpful to some. You can call it what you like—focusing, pondering, "zoning out," "tuning in," "timeout," "quiet time," "minute vacations," or "going to my happy place." In my own life, I have learned (mostly the hard way) that meditation—taking time to think and feel deeply, if even for only a few precious moments—is as vital to my emotional well-being and my spiritual ability to hear the Master as proper nutrition and exercise are to my physical health.

When we relentlessly drive ourselves—often unmercifully—we tend to feel guilty for taking time for ourselves. When the baby is screaming, the toddler is pounding on the bathroom door where you have gone for a moment of respite, or the other children are eerily quiet, which portends of nothing good, you may feel you cannot risk the potential damage to your home, let alone possible harm to life and limb, perhaps the quiet time might last only a nanosecond. Maybe you have only a moment for heartfelt prayer, "Father, please help me hear you over the crying and chaos in our house right now." That doesn't sound too romantic or as spiritual as walking beside still waters, but if we sincerely strive to Hear Him in those very moments when we most need a divine "pep talk," He will speak to us.

Christus by Chad Hawkins

Sometimes, I have been so busy in my life, with work, family, and ecclesiastical responsibilities, that I've hardly had time to breathe. I would rationalize, "I don't have time for meditating now," or, "That isn't a good use of my time." We may even think we are doing nothing when we stop for a moment. Meditation, however, is not doing nothing. It is doing something spiritually significant. It is hard work to listen intently for His voice, to think deeply regarding what He speaks, to thank profoundly for His goodness, and to feel deeply His love. It's hard work to hear Him, but, oh, so worth it when we do.

In my own life, personally, professionally, and ecclesiastically, I have heard Him speak to me in the scriptures (see Doctrine and Covenants 18:33–34). Likewise, I have heard Him in the words of living prophets, Apostles, and women and men leaders who have been called to lead and teach the Saints (see Doctrine and Covenants 1:37–8). We Hear Him at times in His holy house as we worship, serve our kindred dead, and seek for answers to our own questions and solutions to our own struggles. Just as sustaining and strengthening is meditation. For me, that means a drive by myself in the car to clear my head and think aloud. For others, it may be a peaceful walk in nature, some time alone in their room, or prayerful moments in the celestial room of the temple. Whatever the specific means, we all need to affirmatively respond to the Good Shepherd's invitation to spiritually "lie down in green pastures" and "walk beside

Little Fishers of Men by Spencer Rasmussen

As a Little Child by Frank Thomas

the still waters" so we can hear Him, which, in turn, will restore our soul—our devotion to Him, our commitment to the kingdom and our covenants, and our determination to serve Him and our brothers and sisters more thoughtfully. We all need to be restored occasionally so we can do our part in the ongoing Restoration. We all need to focus on Him more. Meditation is focusing on Him. We all need to more conscientiously and consistently tune our ears to Him. Meditation is listening. As we focus and listen, we will indeed hear and learn. I bear witness that the Father and the Son desire to speak peace to our souls, mysteries to our minds, and love to our hearts. Our desire must be to listen to hear His voice—in all the ways whereby He speaks to us. As we do, we will find renewed strength, refortified faith, and greater capacity to love. Oh, how I need all of that and more. That's why I'm trying a little harder each day to hear Him.

"Learn of me, and listen to my words, walk in the meekness of my spirit, and you shall have peace in me" (Doctrine and Covenants 19:23).

This essay is modified from *When You Can't Do it Alone* by Brent L. Top, 2008 © Deseret Book Company. Used with permission.

Prince of Peace by Justin Kunz

Our Own Sacred Grove

BY JACK R.
CHRISTIANSON

For years I had the privilege of taking students to the Sacred Grove and other Church historical sites. That experience allowed me to spend hour after hour pondering Heavenly Father's holy command to young Joseph Smith Jr.: "Hear Him!" Then one day my wife and I found ourselves sitting across a desk from President Henry B. Eyring. He was calling us to preside over an English-speaking mission. We were overwhelmed that the Lord would trust us with such a responsibility. A few weeks later, the specific mission assignment arrived in our mailbox. Again we were overwhelmed and humbled as we read, "You are hereby called to preside over the New York Rochester Mission." We wept together as we went on to read that our assignment included presiding over those same sacred historical sites that we had visited so often.

Early Spring 1820 by Jeffery R Pugh

The Heavens Were Opened by Gary Kapp

The next three years found us entering the Sacred Grove on a regular basis. We preached there, we prayed there, we guided missionaries and family members there. We held zone conferences there. More than any other thing, we were able to recite the Father's sacred words, "Hear Him," numerous times on numerous occasions. These words took on new meaning. They became everything to us. Our quest was and has been to take the time and make the effort to daily Hear Him.

Man of Sorrows by Paul Grass

First Vision by Edmond S. Oliveros

Today, I, personally, Hear Him best while studying the scriptures and the words of living prophets. I Hear Him often while speaking or teaching. I also Hear Him, occasionally, in dreams.

I have learned for myself that Doctrine and Covenants 18:34–36 is true! The Savior said of His words in this scripture,

> These words are not of men nor of man, but of me; wherefore, you shall testify they are of me and not of man;
>
> For it is my voice which speaketh them unto you; for they are given by my Spirit unto you, and by my power you can read them one to another; and save it were by my power you could not have them;
>
> Wherefore, you can testify that you have heard my voice, and know my words.

We hear Him as we heed the words of prophets, seers, and revelators. Ordained Apostles of Jesus Christ always testify of Him. They point the way as we make our way through the heart-wrenching maze of our mortal experiences.

—PRESIDENT RUSSELL M. NELSON

Elder Robert D. Hales taught,

"What a glorious blessing! For when we want to speak to God, we pray. And when we want Him to speak to us, we search the scriptures; for His words are spoken through His prophets. He will then teach us as we listen to the promptings of the Holy Spirit.

"If you have not heard His voice speaking to you lately, return with new eyes and new ears to the scriptures" (Robert D. Hales, "Holy Scriptures: The Power of God unto Our Salvation," *Ensign*, Oct. 2006).

As I search the scriptures and the prophets and apostles, I Hear Him through the words that are written and spoken. Christ taught, "whether by my own voice or by the voice of my servants, it is the same" (D&C 1:38). Elder Bruce R. McConkie wrote, "The Lord and his prophets are one. They are united in the same mind and in the same judgment" (*New Witness for the Articles of Faith*, [Salt Lake City: Deseret Book, 1985], 1). Truly, it has been a glorious experience to Hear Him through His chosen prophets or to read answers to my many prayers in the scriptures!

I Hear Him, at times, while speaking or teaching by the power of the Holy Ghost. The Spirit puts His words into my mind and heart and tells me what to say. "Therefore, verily I say unto you, lift up your voices unto this people; speak the thoughts that I shall put into your hearts" (D&C 100:5). I Hear Him, from time to time, while dreaming. Usually, the dream is about someone I know, love, and respect. The Lord knows I will listen to certain people more than others. Therefore, at times, I dream of specific people who teach me or speak to me. Sometimes, it is to give correction. At other times, it comes with such sweetness and lovingkindness that I awake and find myself crying. Other times, I awake with a feeling of unspeakable peace. The words

Jesús and Disciples by Rose Kathleen Peterson

of Job 33:14–16 have had great meaning to me when it comes to the Lord's command to Hear Him:

"For God speaketh once, yea twice, yet man perceiveth it not.

"In a dream, in a vision of the night, when deep sleep falleth upon me, in slumberings upon the bed;

"Then he openeth the ears of men, and sealeth their instruction."

I have learned that none of us have to visit the Sacred Grove in order to Hear Him. Though I have spent many, many hours in that holy place and was called to preside over it for three years, I had heard Him many times before walking into the shade of its trees. Hearing Him through prophets, scriptures, giving talks, teaching, and sometimes through dreams has allowed my testimony to grow into its own mighty forest.

The Spirit of God Like a Fire Is Burning by Anne Marie Oborn

Through His Light by Kate Lee

Listening, Doing, and Sharing

BY RICHARD J. ALLEN

The Pattern of Hearing the Lord, Obeying His Counsel, and Testifying to Others about the Truths of His Gospel Plan

In the early spring of 1820, the young Joseph Smith was impressed to follow the counsel of James in the New Testament about how to discern gospel truths: **"If any of you lack wisdom, let him ask of God, that giveth to all men liberally, and upbraideth not; and it shall be given him" (James 1:5).** The young Joseph retired to a quiet grove of trees not far from his home—similar to his mother's pattern of praying in a natural outdoor setting—and offered a sublime prayer for divine wisdom. What then occurred was a cosmic event that opened the Restoration of the Church in the latter days: "[A pillar of

First Vision from Above by James L. Johnson

What wisdom do you lack? What do you feel an urgent need to know or understand? Follow the example of the Prophet Joseph. Find a quiet place where you can regularly go. Humble yourself before God. Pour out your heart to your Heavenly Father. Turn to Him for answers and for comfort.

—PRESIDENT RUSSELL M. NELSON

light] no sooner appeared than I found myself delivered from the enemy which held me bound. When the light rested upon me I saw two Personages, whose brightness and glory defy all description, standing above me in the air. One of them spake unto me, calling me by name and said, pointing to the other—This is My Beloved Son. Hear Him!" (Joseph Smith—History 1:17).

That verse from the Pearl of Great Price was the most frequently referenced scriptural passage shared during the April 2020 general conference, being cited no fewer than twelve times by conference speakers (and thus more often than any other passage in any conference session over the past decade). The passage was cited in full by President Russell M. Nelson in footnote 1 of his speech entitled "Go Forward in Faith." In addition, two short segments from the Joseph Smith—History passage were also quoted frequently by various speakers during the April conference: "This is My Beloved Son. Hear Him!" (quoted four times, including twice by President Nelson) and "Hear Him" (quoted seven times, including once by President Nelson).

That glorious statement during the First Vision—"This is My Beloved Son. Hear Him!"—became the enduring scriptural emblem of the Restoration to unfold in its majesty through the visitation of additional angelic ministers. These additional ministers acted under the power of the heavens as an eternal blessing to all the sons and daughters of God in the latter days leading toward the Second Coming of the Lord. As President Nelson confirmed in his final talk during the Sunday afternoon session of the April conference, the two words *Hear Him* serve as a key token of the Lord's counsel for all of us to follow faithfully, day by day.

When we focus on the pattern of listening, doing, and sharing, we can also remind ourselves of the inspiring scriptural words from the Lord that include the key action word *do* as in this memorable passage of divine counsel: "**If ye know these things, happy are ye if ye do them**" **(John 15:17)**. Consider and apply also the additional memorable *do* word passages from the Savior given to us in 3 Nephi 27:21–22 and D&C 11:12.

I am forever grateful to my parents for their examples of how to hear the Lord and perform and share the essence of His divine purposes. When I was but ten years old, my mother passed away giving birth to my younger brother, Robert. She left for me a personally signed copy of the Book of Mormon as a precious font of truth for my coming years of growth and service in listening to, doing, and sharing the truths of the Savior's gospel. Many years later, shortly after my marriage to Carol Lynn, and on the eve of starting a family of our own, I asked my father to give me a father's blessing. This being a patriarchal privilege, he prepared himself during a long period of fasting and prayer and then bestowed upon me a wonderful blessing containing many words of personal encouragement and counsel, somewhat in the uplifting spirit of the Prophet Joseph Smith's account of the First Vision in 1820. At the conclusion of the blessing, my father shared an inspiring image that can be shared with others because of its universal application: "And now, my beloved son, as you journey forth into the uncertain world, reach up your hands to the lap of God. And if you will do this, He will lead you, He will guide you, save, and exalt you in the eternal worlds."

Was This for Me?
by Tammi Lunt Iba

I have pondered countless times over the years how well this image reflects the true spirit of meekness and humility so essential to devoted discipleship that is based on hearing the counsel of the Lord directly and taking steps to act upon it and share it with others—the essence of the pattern of listening, doing, and sharing. Similarly, fathers and mothers can tell uplifting stories to their children and grandchildren and seek inspiration from on high to find the most effective imagery and gifts for expressing true principles in such a way that the rising generation will choose to hear the Lord personally and make wise choices that enlighten them and many others.

I Know That My Savior Loves Me by Rebecca Johnston

Hear Him | Listening, Doing, and Sharing

Bearing a Child in Her Arms (Mary and the Christ Child) by Elspeth C. Young

Years ago, as a green, young art student, I struggled to capture a difficult subject on canvas. My art professor joined me at my easel, and though he saw my struggle, he did not grab an oil-tipped brush, fix my impasse, and saunter away omnisciently triumphant. Instead, he reassuringly said, "If you look at anything hard enough, you can figure it out."

While it was sound art instruction, I've found these words apply equally to my quest to find Christ "in and through all things" (D&C 88:6). I often Hear Him best with my eyes, and indeed, if I look hard enough, there He always is, in sunshine or shadow, my best times or worst—His arms of mercy are extended, ready to lift, comfort, strengthen, and steady.

Ironically, however, there are seldom times more difficult for me to see Him than when I'm endeavoring to paint Him. I sometimes feel like an artistic Peter—unable to see His outstretched hand and compassionate countenance amidst the multitude of blurring waves that surge around my creativity. Questions pester; worries abound; opinions distract.

But if, like Peter, I cry out for Him and "look hard enough," He is there. True, answers may only come in the fourth watch, after I have expended all my puny emotional and physical strength to solve a creative storm. But answers do come, and with the artistic answers, I come to know Him better.

My father, Al Young, has always said, "Our gifts and abilities are simply places where Heaven's veil has been rubbed thin, and when we use our gifts—no matter how exquisite the journey—it is simply a path to knowing the Creator better."

As "one of the least of these," I can plainly, confidently, and sincerely testify of the Personal Messiah: personal to every single son and daughter of God—mighty to console, to help, to save. Jaweh (Jehovah) means "I am always here for you," and I have found that to be perfectly true—like Him.

—ELSPETH C. YOUNG

Does God really want to speak to you? Yes! "As well might man stretch forth his puny arm to stop the Missouri river in its decreed course . . . as to hinder the Almighty from pouring down knowledge from heaven upon the heads of the Latter-day Saints.

—PRESIDENT RUSSELL M. NELSON

Hearing the Voice of the Lord

BY HEIDI S. SWINTON

Over forty years ago, a tall, grave-faced doctor walked into my hospital room, sat down in the plastic bucket chair next to my bed, and took my hand. He looked at me for a few moments. We'd met just the day before when I came into the hospital at 2 a.m. pregnant with twins and in labor at seven months. My doctor had retired, and this high-risk specialist had taken over my case.

There I was, a young mother with one son who had just died and another son who was fighting for his life on a respirator. Two months premature, he couldn't breathe, and he had a hole in his heart and a litany of other problems. After miscarrying five babies, I had seen these twins as a blessing to make up for all the heartache and broken dreams. Now I was facing even deeper loss and disappointment.

I will never forget what the doctor said. "Heidi, I want you to know this. You have one son all the way home. That may be no comfort to you right now, but, believe me, in the years ahead, you will come to understand and know what it means. I have a teenage son, and I wonder if I will get him all the way home. Yours is already there." Over the days and weeks that followed, many friends called and came to see me and sent flowers and beautiful cards. But it was those words, "all the way home," that made the difference.

The doctor was speaking, but it was the Lord I was hearing. In Doctrine and Covenants 1:38 we are told, "Whether by mine own voice or by the voice of my servants, it is the same." The truth of eternal life borne to me that day was a spiritual witness from God. In the depths of my grief, the voice of the Lord sounded in my ears. "All the way home" spoke volumes to me then; it continues to speak to me today.

I count much of my life from the experience of the death of my eldest son. It was then that I really began to understand personal revelation. The questions "Why?" and "How could this happen?" begged for answers, yet my soul searched for more than just resolution. Suddenly mortality took on a different dimension,

I Have Succored Thee by Mary Brickey

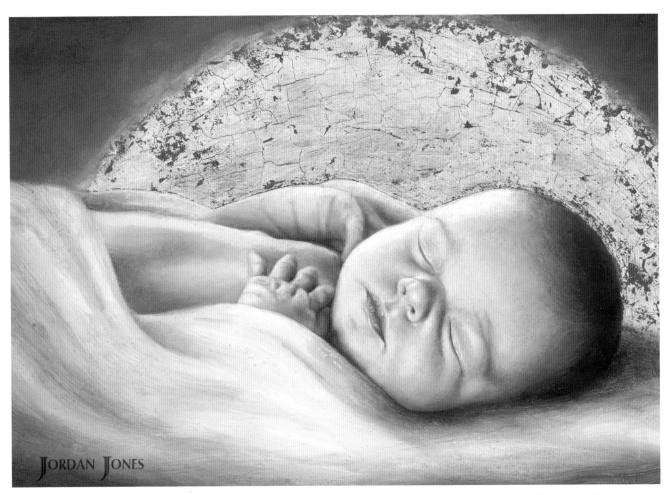

JORDAN JONES

Unto Us a Son Is Given
by Jordan Jones

became part of the plan but not all of it. Eternal glory and its promises now included a face and a name: Christian Horne Swinton. To be with him, I needed to get all the way home myself—to see that his twin brother, Cameron—who lived—and the three brothers who followed, made it home as well.

That focus didn't require a U-turn in my late twenties or even a sharp turn. He called for me to increase my willingness and my ability to have ears to hear, to listen. At one time, all of us knew the Lord's voice. We cheered in the premortal existence when Christ presented the Father's plan. We heard it there; we are living it here. I have no doubt that we are tied to the heavens by revelation. We sometimes call that spiritual tie "being in tune."

President Joseph F. Smith, sixth president of the Church, said of his own experience receiving revelation: "I fervently believe that God has manifested to me in my present capacity, many glorious things, many principles and oftentimes much more wisdom than is inherent in myself; and I believe He will continue

In Awe of Him by Paul Mann

to do so as long as I am receptive, as long as I am in a position to hear when He speaks, to listen when He calls, and to receive when He gives to me that which He desires" (Joseph Fielding Smith, *Origins of the Reorganized Church* (pamphlet), [Salt Lake City: Deseret News Press, 1909]). These important steps put revelation within the reach of each one of us: be receptive, be in the right position to hear, listen, and receive when he speaks.

What stands in our way of receiving? In the Doctrine and Covenants 66:10, we are counseled: "Seek not to be cumbered." *Cumbered* is a good word to contrast with *come*. *Cumbered* sounds weighted down with purses full of problems, programs, wants, needs, responsibilities, challenges. Every day we have long lists of things to do. Do this or that, come to this and drop off that, stop here, pick up there . . . you know the list. Fractured lives that live by the needs of the

Every woman and every man who makes covenants with God and keeps those covenants, and who participates worthily in priesthood ordinances, has direct access to the power of God.

—PRESIDENT RUSSELL M. NELSON

The Light and Life of the World by Cynthia Dye

Christ
by Boston Madsen

day have no peace. How can we hear the Good Shepherd's voice in our hearts when the Spirit has to take a number just to get on our day's list? *Come* means, "Lay aside the things of this world," as the Lord said to Emma Smith, "and seek for the things of a better" (D&C 25:10).

During the delivery, Christian had suffered from a brain hemorrhage, and tests had shown that the damage was severe. "He will never be able to run and walk like his twin brother may," the doctors had informed my husband at the hospital across town from mine, where he held vigil over our newly born sons, "but we may be able to keep him alive." Jeff asked if there was somewhere he could go to be alone. They showed him to a small office. He knelt and poured out his feelings to his Father in Heaven. He spoke of our righteous hopes for a family, and then he said, "But if Christian's work is done, we are ready to accept that." He walked out of the office and over to the Isolette where Christian lay. The signal on the heart monitor flattened out. Christian had heard the voice as did Peter, "Come." Come all the way home.

Several days later in the cemetery, we heard the voice of the Lord in our hearts—a still, small voice spoke of peace and a promise found in John, "Peace I leave with you, my peace I give unto you: not as the world giveth, give I unto you. Let not your heart be troubled, neither let it be afraid" (John 14:27).

This essay has been modified from "Hearing the Voice of the Lord" by Heidi S. Swinton, found in *May Christ Lift Thee Up: Talks from the 1998 Women's Conference Sponsored by Brigham Young University and the Relief Society*, 1999 © Deseret Book Company. Used with permission.

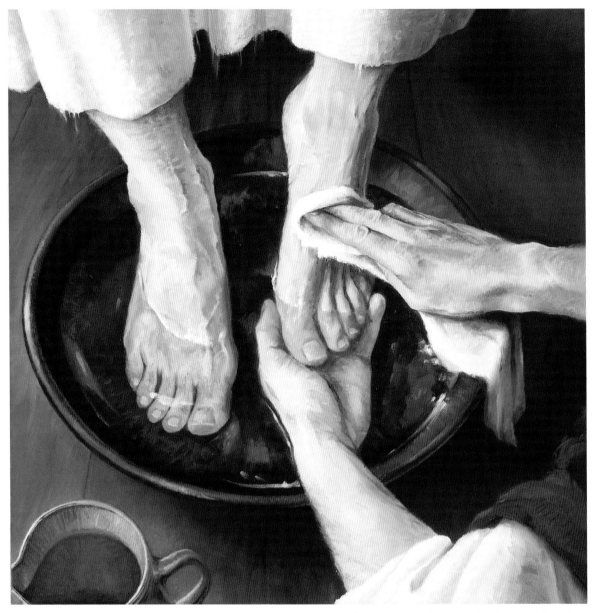

Jesus Washes an Apostle's Feet by Laurie Lisonbee

Our promise to always remember the Savior gives us strength to stand for truth and righteousness—whether we are in a large crowd or in our solitary places, where no one knows our actions except for God. When we remember Him and His name we bear, we have no place for self-degrading comparisons or overbearing judgments. With our eyes on the Savior, we see ourselves for who we really are—a cherished child of God.

—SISTER LISA L. HARKNESS

As a Hen Gathereth by Jeff Hein

Mother—A Precious and Chosen Vessel by Megan Rieker

Prayer

BY ERIC D. HUNTSMAN

One of my favorite examples of prayer from the Old Testament is not that of a patriarch or a prophet but of a heartbroken woman. Suffering because of her barrenness, Hannah prepared herself to seek the Lord by fasting and going to the tabernacle at Shiloh, where she could find space for worship near God's presence. She then wordlessly poured out her heart to the Lord: "She was in bitterness of soul, and prayed unto the Lord, and wept sore. And she vowed a vow, and said, O Lord of hosts, if thou wilt indeed look on the affliction of thine handmaid, and remember me, and not forget thine handmaid, but wilt give unto thine handmaid a man child, then I will give him unto the Lord all the days of his life. . . . Now Hannah, she spake in her heart; only her lips moved, but her voice was not heard" (1 Samuel 1:10–13).

Hannah's silent prayer was indeed answered, and she conceived and gave birth to the future prophet Samuel. In gratitude, she offered a beautiful prayer of

The Lord's Prayer by Ryan S. Brown

Gethsemane by James C. Christensen

Be Still and Know That I Am by Darin Ashby

thanks (1 Samuel 2:1–10) and later dedicated her son to the Lord's service as she had promised. Because Hannah's experience was so deeply personal, we can closely relate to it, seeing how we should pour out both our desires and our heartaches to the Lord, express thankfulness when our prayers are heard, and then act afterwards, sometimes at great sacrifice, thereby worshipping Him with our strength as well as with our minds and hearts.

Jesus Himself was a model of prayer, praying regularly throughout His ministry. His example and teachings help us understand how we should prepare for

Pray in the name of Jesus Christ about your concerns, your fears, your weaknesses—yes, the very longings of your heart. And then listen!

—PRESIDENT RUSSELL M. NELSON

prayer, what kinds of things we should pray for, and how we should follow our prayers by serving God more intently afterward. For instance, Jesus taught us to prepare ourselves for prayer by directing us to pray in places and in ways that allow us to focus on God rather than seeking the attention of others. Unlike hypocrites who pray to be heard by others, He directed His followers, "When thou prayest, *enter into thy closet*, and when thou hast shut thy door, pray to thy Father which is in secret; and thy Father which seeth in secret shall reward thee openly" (Matthew 6:6; emphasis added).

Prayer is a natural human impulse, one that brings great spiritual comfort and power to God's children regardless of their religious affiliation or beliefs. As a result, even though proper authority and important truths about God were lost in the centuries after Jesus and His apostles left the earth, prayer remained a central part of Jewish and Christian worship. Similarly, when the new religion of Islam arose, it drew upon Jewish and Christian precedents and likewise emphasized the importance of prayer. After the Middle Ages, the Protestant Reformation further emphasized the importance of personal prayer and changed how people prayed, setting the stage in many ways for the Restoration. Despite our differences with these different traditions, when we see what we have in common with our fellow believers, we can be encouraged in our own prayers and can even learn from the examples of our friends of other faiths and strive to improve our own prayers by praying with more reverence, concentration, and devotion.

Latter-day Saints' understanding of prayer and experience with it have been shaped by the restored gospel of Jesus Christ. The Restoration began with a sincere, personal prayer. In Joseph Smith's 1838 account of the First Vision, canonized as Joseph Smith—History 1:8–20 (*Histories, 1832–1844, Joseph Smith Papers*, [Salt Lake City: Church Historian's Press, 2012], 204–19),[1] we learn how the young Joseph's concern over which church he should join led

---

1 See also Richard L. Bushman, *Joseph Smith, Rough Stone Rolling*, (New York: Vintage, 2005), 22–27, and Steven C. Harper, *Joseph Smith's First Vision: A Guide to the Historical Accounts*, (Salt Lake City: Deseret Book, 2012), 18–22.

Gethsemane by Larry Conrad Winborg

1820 by Kendal Ray Johnson

him to act upon the promise of James 1:5 that if anyone lacks wisdom, they should ask of God. Feeling that he certainly needed divine guidance, this boy of fourteen retired to a secluded place in the woods one day in the spring of 1820—seeking space, spiritual and mental, as much as finding an actual physical place—to make an attempt. Even though he came from a Bible-reading family that regularly prayed together,[2] Joseph nevertheless recorded, **"It was the first time in my life that I had made such an attempt, for amidst all my anxieties, I had never as yet made the attempt to pray vocally" (Joseph Smith—History 1:14).** Despite his newness to prayer and in spite of demonic opposition, the young Joseph persevered and received a vision of the Father and the Son, informing him that he should not join any of the existing churches, thus laying the groundwork for the restoration of the gospel of Jesus Christ (Steven C. Harper, *Joseph Smith's First Vision: A Guide to the Historical Accounts*, [Salt Lake City: Deseret Book, 2012], 27–30).

Our real, intimate relationship with the Lord should lead us to want to be with him often, not only to speak with him in formal prayer but also to enjoy his presence spiritually throughout the day. Restoration scripture, particularly the Book of Mormon, reaffirms the importance of praying frequently while also teaching that being prayerful is as much an attitude or way of living given that one cannot pray continuously, at least not verbally. Sometimes informal prayers, offered while involved in another activity such as working or driving, can be the occasions of some of our most needed communication with God. Just being still so we can feel His Spirit is part of being prayerful.

Alma pleaded, "Humble yourselves before the Lord, and call on his holy name, and watch and pray continually, that ye may not be tempted above that which ye can bear, and thus be led by the Holy Spirit, becoming humble, meek, submissive, patient, full of love and all long-suffering; having faith on the Lord; having a hope that ye shall receive eternal life; having the love of God always in your hearts, that ye may be lifted up at the last day and enter into his rest" (Alma 13:28–29).

This essay is modified from *Worship* by Eric D. Huntsman, 2016 © Deseret Book Company. Used with permission.

---

2 Lucy Mack Smith, *The Revised and Enhanced History of Joseph Smith by His Mother*, edited by Scot Facer Proctor and Maurine Jensen Proctor, (Salt Lake City: Bookcraft, 1996), 47–48, records that Joseph's mother, Lucy Mack Smith, naturally turned to fervent prayer during a dangerous sickness. See also Richard L. Bushman, *Joseph Smith, Rough Stone Rolling*, (New York: Vintage, 2005), 11–14.

Bind Up the Brokenhearted by Sandy Freckleton Gagon

I have long enjoyed depicting the glory, beauty, and perfection of the human form, for I consider it to be the supreme creation of God, created in His image.

It is His Atonement, death, and Resurrection that stand at the center of my faith and belief.

—KENT GOODLIFFE

The Light by Kent Goodliffe

Bind Up the Brokenhearted

BY SANDY
FRECKLETON
GAGON

For me, the inspiration for my paintings is often combinations of my own life experiences. The following quote spoke deeply to me. Robert L. Millet said, "The cosmic Christ who creates and redeems worlds without number is the same gentle and good Shepherd who goes in search of one wandering lamb. He who holds all things in his power is the same who stills the storms of the human heart by a healing touch" (*Alive in Christ: The Miracle of Spiritual Rebirth*, [Salt Lake City: Deseret Book, 1997], 34).

Indeed, President Howard W. Hunter observed that "whatever Jesus lays his hands upon lives. If Jesus lays his hands upon a marriage, it lives. If he is allowed to lay his hands on the family, it lives" ("Reading the Scriptures," *Ensign*, Nov. 1979).

God has never promised us a life of ease or an existence free from strain and anxiety. We have not been promised that we will be spared bitter potions in this life. But we have been assured that we are not alone and if we trust in and rely

on His mighty arm, we will be empowered and comforted in our trials; we will eventually be delivered out of bondage (see Mosiah 24:14).

In September 2014, in the midst of overwhelming adversity in my own life, I completed the painting *Bind Up the Brokenhearted*; it was a way of expressing

Jesus Said to Her, "Mary"
by William Whitaker

Come Follow Me by Brent Borup

my testimony. I wanted to share my feelings about the Atonement and how Christ is there to succor us through the challenges we face in mortality. I know Jesus is the Christ, the Son of the Living God. And I know we can Hear Him.

I saw the painting in my mind before I started it. I wanted a piece that would represent all who have been broken in life and the Savior, who is the Master Healer!

There are many beautiful paintings depicting Christ and a white lamb, some of which are symbolic of His eventual Atonement as the sacrificial lamb.

However, I wanted to depict a lamb who had experienced the adversities of life. The wool on the lamb was bloody and torn. He looked how I felt. I wanted to convey that the Savior rescues us and has power over the elements. He is not bound by time or the myriad challenges we face in life.

He has already walked that path and knows how to guide us over the pitfalls. He calls us by name, one by one, if we will Hear Him.

I only paint from live models; however, I didn't want a lamb in my studio, so I took my model to a rescue shelter for farm animals, though I didn't know it was a rescue shelter until after I'd had this sacred experience. My model, who was in full costume, and I found the corral where several lambs lived. He asked me what I wanted him to do. I encouraged him to go into the pen and pick up a lamb, and then I would shoot photographic reference. He gently replied that he needed me to go ask the farmer what the lamb's name was. I hurried back to the barn and asked Farmer Gil the lamb's name; he replied, "Gizmo." After I told my model the lamb's name, he again asked me what I wanted him to do. "Just go in and pick up the lamb."

At this point, my model taught me something profound. "No, Sandy," he said. "It wouldn't be right to just go in and pick up the lamb." He said he needed to spend time with Gizmo. My model, clothed as the Savior, then sat on a bale of hay and called to the lamb. He drew Gizmo to him through love and kindness. He stroked the back of the lamb's neck and head. He spent over half an hour speaking to him, calling him by name, and gently caressing the lamb. He then invited Gizmo to be in the painting. I would have never thought of any of this.

I was deeply struck with the overwhelming feeling that this is how the Savior treats each of us; He draws us to Him by name . . . one by one. He calms us, enfolds us in His arms, and heals our broken hearts.

When my model finally picked up Gizmo, the lamb was perfectly still and at peace.

Later, when we were finished, I went to my car, and the whole experience replayed in my mind. Tears streamed down my face, and I felt I had experienced a very sacred event, as if the Savior had been present and I had heard Him.

Son of Man
by Bruce Cheever

This painting is centered around the atonement of Jesus Christ, containing symbolism from events and circumstances of His life. Isaiah's prophetic and poetic words described Christ's sacrifice when he declared: "Surely he hath borne our griefs, and carried our sorrows . . . and with his stripes we are healed" Isaiah 53:4, 5.

—BRUCE CHEEVER

Road to Emmaus by Wendy Keller

Christ Appearing to the Eleven by Scott Snow

Praising His Amazing Grace

BY SCOTT
SORENSEN

As President Russell M. Nelson and others have greatly emphasized the invitation to Hear Him, I've been asking myself, "Why? Why do I want to Hear Him? What difference would it make in my life?" I have learned that I will not do something or study something unless I value it. So I've had to determine what value there is in hearing Him. Let me share with you how hearing Him has made all the difference for me as I have personally wrestled with anxiety and depression for over twenty-five years.

As a teenager, I felt mentally weak and very lonely. I desperately struggled with feelings of inadequacy, failure, and worthlessness. I often felt like other people were better off without me in their lives. Though I fought these dark feelings, I remember memorizing Ether 12:27 in seminary and being inspired by the promise that God's grace could make my weaknesses become strengths.

Peter's Faith in Christ
by Mark R. Pugh

My assumption was that if I had enough faith, God would heal my mind so I wouldn't have to suffer anymore through the dark and self-defeating thoughts that constantly surrounded me.

Over the next ten years, I graduated high school, served a full-time mission, got married in the temple, had three kids, and graduated from college. But my anxiety and depression seemed to only get deeper and darker. What did God want from me? Why was I suffering so much? Why was He performing miracles in others' lives but not mine? Was I being punished for past sins? Did I need to be perfect first? Though Ether 12:27 had given me a glimmer of hope all those years ago, at this point in my life, I firmly believed that verse was not true for me. I didn't feel much strength, mostly weakness.

After college graduation, I suffered a major, devastating career setback. It completely wrecked me. The bits of light I had been desperately hanging onto quickly faded, and two months later, I felt like the light was gone. One day, I was eating lunch in my car at an abandoned mall parking lot. I cried out to God, "Where are you? Why won't you help me? I can't do this anymore! I've done all that you've asked, and I feel nothing but sad and hopeless." Then I said two words to Him I've never said before, "I'm done!"

A few minutes later, with tears streaming down my face, I had a deep impression and felt God's voice say, "You have depression because it makes you a more compassionate person."

What? I was confused.

The impression came again. "You have depression because it makes you a more compassionate person."

After my mind caught hold of this thought, a second impression came. "And I need you to be compassionate for what I want you to do in life."

Whoa!

Christ by Melissa Misurelli

These two distinct but connected impressions filled me. I felt loved. Like, really, really loved.

"You have depression because it makes you a more compassionate person, and I need you to be compassionate for what I want you to do in life."

Gethsemane's Path by Steve McGinty

You know those moments in life where you have a thousand thoughts run through your head in a split second? That was what happened to me next. It had never occurred to me that anxiety and depression served me in any way. I always felt like they were the master and I was the servant. It had never occurred to me that my struggles had any meaning. I always felt like my suffering was pointless, needless, a punishment. It had never occurred to me that God was okay with my depression. Honestly, it had never occurred to me that it was okay to have depression at all. I had always thought it was the ugly part of me that needed to be removed, not the beautiful part of me that needed to be embraced. Now, all of a sudden, I felt

Gethsemane by Douglas Fryer

Hear Him by Steven Lloyd Neal

purpose for my pain. My suffering meant something. In an almost paradoxical way, I finally realized my suffering was actually the source of my power!

Peace and purpose for my pain are exactly what God gave me that day. Peace to know that it's okay to have depression. Purpose to know that my depression allows profound compassion to flow through me to others.

Because of this Hear Him experience, Paul's testimony is now my testimony: "*And he said unto me, My grace is sufficient for thee: for my strength is made perfect in weakness. Most gladly therefore will I rather glory in my infirmities, that the power of Christ may rest upon me. Therefore I take pleasure in infirmities . . . for when I am weak, then am I made strong* (2 Corinthians 12:9–10; italics added).

Now I understand a far deeper meaning to Ether 12:27. In high school, I thought strength was what you had in the absence of weakness. Now I know that as we accept our weakness and trust in God anyway, He can make strength flow through us in beautiful and creative ways. I am stronger in mortality because I am weak. Depression is my superpower! I praise God that He allows us to Hear Him, and I praise God for His amazing grace!

The Identifying Power of Christ

BY ANTHONY
SWEAT

The Book of Mormon introduces us to a wonderful term, the condescension of Christ (2 Nephi 4:26). *Condescend* means to come down from a high station to a low station, or "to descend to a less formal or dignified level"; "to waive the privileges of rank" (Merriam-Webster's Eleventh Collegiate Dictionary [Springfield, MA: Merriam-Webster, 2003], s.v. "condescend"). Condescension in a worldly sense would be like Celine Dion happily singing harmony in your fledgling ward choir. In heavenly terms, condescension is God agreeing to leave his exalted station in heaven, waiving his privileges as a member of the Godhead, and descending to the lowliest of stations on earth—born as a helpless baby in a dirty cave in a backward town to an impoverished and obscure family in a politically oppressed nation.

From the moment Jesus wrapped his celestial spirit in telestial flesh he became like us in his mortality. Like all of us, our Lord experienced the veil of forgetfulness. Jesus had to learn he was Jehovah. When did He realize He was special, was the Messiah? We don't really know. It is evident by the time He was twelve years old, in the temple, that He already understood who His Father was and that His life's purpose was to do God's will (see Luke 2:49). Despite this knowledge, however, Jesus continued to develop as a regular boy. He likely ran footraces and lost as often as He won. His mind was brilliant, for sure, but perhaps He forgot things. The story of when He was twelve at the temple is evidence of that as He overlooked telling His parents where He was, causing an unnecessary three-day search for a missing boy. There's no sin in any of this. It was just part of His physical, mental, social, and spiritual development, which Jesus had to experience as He grew into a man (see Luke 2:52). None of what I have written here implies any impropriety in God's Divine Son. It implies mortality.

Jesus not only experienced mortal life as we do, but He also experienced temptation as we do, in all its difficulty. The Lord felt the tugs of temptation

Little Shepherdess by Cheryl Ann Betenson

Even in the midst of unique trials and challenges, we are truly blessed!

—PRESIDENT DALLIN H. OAKS

Thy Will Be Done by Travis Wood

on His divine robe and had to reject its pulls, just like the rest of us. He had to resist feelings of pride and selfishness—the most common of all human vices. Jesus faced the usual temptations of dishonesty, deceit, laziness, lust, anger, overindulgence, and the like. Speaking from empathy and not sympathy, the Lord said in the Doctrine and Covenants that He is "Jesus Christ, your advocate, *who knoweth the weakness of man* and how to succor them who are tempted" (D&C 62:1; emphasis added).

Jesus's empathy, however, extends beyond the experience and suffering of a normal human being—even beyond that of any mortal. When Jesus crossed the brook Cedron and entered the Garden of Gethsemane late that fateful Passover night, He crossed a threshold beyond any human experience, into something only He could endure and none of us could imagine. It is suffering so intense that in the only firsthand account given by Jesus of His atoning anguish, the Savior doesn't even finish the sentence: "Which suffering caused myself, even God, the greatest of all, to tremble because of pain, and to bleed at every pore, and to suffer both body and spirit—and would that I might not drink the bitter cup, and shrink—" (D&C 19:18). The Savior leaves off telling

Gethsemane Grove
by Derek J. Hegsted

Christ frequented the grove often, as the scriptures state. The painting represents Christ's connection with every living thing.

Envisioning that the Savior had a hand in the planting of Gethsemane personalized it to me. The scattering of the seeds of flowers and especially the red anemones is such a personal, pleasing thought.

—DEREK HEGSTED

Intercession by David Lindsley

Because of His profound and eternal love, Jesus Christ suffered and died for you and me. He broke open the gates of death, shattered the barriers that separated friends and loved ones, and brought hope to the hopeless, healing to the sick, and deliverance to the captive.

—ELDER DIETER F. UCHTDORF

us about a suffering we mortals couldn't comprehend even if the Son of God explained it.

Did Jesus *literally* experience all the happenings of humanity on that night? When speaking with Robert L. Millet, former dean of Religious Education at BYU, on this subject, he said to me, "Did Jesus really suffer delivery pains in Gethsemane? Did He suffer an ACL tear? Did He receive a rejection letter from Stanford? Or, rather, is it the case that His perfect empathy comes out of his perfect love?" That is a great question.

Whatever the answer may be, the gospel reality is that a connection was made that night through the Lord's infinite suffering to each of us who suffer.

The scriptures are clear that Jesus suffered for all of us so He can empathetically guide us. *Succor* is the word often used, meaning "to give assistance or aid." Paul says, "For in that he himself hath suffered being tempted, he is able to succour them that are tempted" (Hebrews 2:18). Thus, because Jesus has successfully suffered and overcome *all* things, He can help us in *our* things. That is why His day-to-day mortal experience became a necessary part of His day-to-day saving divinity; it makes the Lord our ultimate Counselor.

If we exercise faith in Him, each of us may have the profound knowledge that our Savior perfectly knows us, loves us, understands us, and is with us in our day-to-day lives. As He promises us in the Doctrine and Covenants, "I will go before your face. I will be on your right hand and on your left, and my Spirit shall be in your hearts, and mine angels round about you, to bear you up" (D&C 84:88). He can bear us up now because He bore all things before.

This essay is modified from *Christ in Every Hour* by Anthony Sweat, 2016 © Deseret Book Company. Used with permission.

And trials are necessary for us to be shaped and made fit to receive that happiness that comes as we qualify for the greatest of all the gifts of God. . . . For each, the power of deliverance is available — not to escape the test but to endure it well.

—PRESIDENT HENRY B. EYRING

Call of the Master by Kelsy and Jesse Lightweave

"And I will give thee the treasures of darkness, and hidden riches of secret places, that thou mayest know that I, the Lord, which call thee by thy name, am the God of Israel" (Isaiah 45:3).

When the call comes . . . will we be ready to seek the hidden riches? Can we Hear Him?

Realizing that we all have busy lives, we often find it hard to see beyond the tasks at hand. We can become so busy, that tasks start to become perfunctory in nature. In the midst of the tumult, it frequently comes—when least expected: the call to do something greater. *The Call of the Master* is to remind us of time, work, and the purpose of our earthly experience.

The turbulence of the waters surrounding our boat is often a reflection of ourselves. Our focus in life will dictate how distracting the waves become. Hopefully, we can make time to calm the waters surrounding our busy endeavors, reflect upon existence, and, perhaps, see the Savior standing along the shore, ready to issue His call. And we can Hear Him.

—KELSY AND JESSE LIGHTWEAVE

Losing My Hearing and Gaining a Sure Knowledge of God

BY LISA HALVERSON

Last year I became 100 percent, totally deaf. The loss of all natural sound, the reliance on assistive devices to hear and comprehend, and the experience of struggling to hear those around me have increased the importance and relevance to me of scriptures about hearing the voice of the Lord.

I have experienced the terrifying fear of losing all natural sound. No longer recognizing my husband's voice. Never knowing what my son's voice would sound like after puberty hit and the first crack came. No longer discerning between my daughter's laugh and her cry. Never hearing a grandbaby's gurgle. For these losses and potential losses, I have sobbed into my pillow at night. And it was only after a powerful experience with the Spirit, which gave me a sure knowledge of the reality of the Resurrection, that I was able to say, "Thy will be done."

Hearing loss has made me a very skilled and dedicated *listener*. I wish I could say it has also made me amazingly attuned to spiritually hearing the voice of the Lord, but I still have a long way to go. Hearing loss has piqued my interest in studying the themes "hearing" and "listening" in scriptures. Here are a few core themes I have noticed.

Difference between Hearing and Understanding

One thing someone may realize when they are deaf or hard of hearing is the significant difference between hearing and listening. If one has normal hearing, they *hear* without much effort. Even *I* hear quite a bit of sound through my cochlear implants—it just doesn't always make meaningful sense! Hearing is easy!

But *listening* and the *understanding* that comes from it are hard work—listening requires time and focus and empathy and the ability to be more intent on the other person than on our own next response. The Lord does not want us to only *hear* His word, but He also wants us to *listen* to it intently, to *understand* His meaning, and to *obey* His guidance.

Refuge by Mandy Jane Williams

For me, revelation comes while I'm on my feet working.

A new painting begins with an idea, such as an overall color scheme, a certain grouping of figures, or a particular gesture that evokes a certain feeling I am after. I rarely, if ever, see the finished painting in my mind before I begin. Mostly it is that overall impression with out the details spelled out. As I work with my models and struggle through design choices the painting reveals itself to me slowly one piece at a time. I work and try to flesh out how to capture that initial impression. I try to feel my way, seeking to hear those still, small impressions. Often it is a feeling that something isn't quite right yet. The feel of the piece isn't quite what I'm after. At times, I have found it helpful to get away from the painting. I'll take a break and put it away for a while. When I come back to it I'll sit quietly and think of ways I can make the painting better. That quiet time with the painting helps me to discern what the painting needs. Ideas will come to mind on how to improve upon whats been done, or on what the work needs to bring it to a finish. Sometimes major revisions are needed. Major changes can cause me to dig deep and summon courage. Other times I can see that only small things are needed to refine the piece and add that finishing touch. Sometimes the inspiration is to tone down/simplify a passage to enhance the focal area. I feel it's a lot like Nephi's description as he was building the boat. "And the Lord did show me from time to time after what manner I should work the timbers of the ship." (1 Nephi 18:1) I know the Lord helps us as we seek His guidance in our work. Especially when we are engaged in blessing His children.

—MICHAEL MALM

Sometimes I have treated receiving revelation as if it should be as effortless as hearing sound is for those with perfect hearing. But receiving revelation is an exercise not in hearing but in understanding meaning. It requires preparation and work. And that requires listening.

Preparing the "Acoustics"

I do a *lot* of work to ensure that I understand the people around me.

Do I make the same efforts to "prepare the acoustics" when listening to God? Do I take time to listen to Him before I jump into the noisy environments of

And He Opened His Mouth and Taught Them by Michael Malm

Why Would You Do This for Me? by Susan Edwards

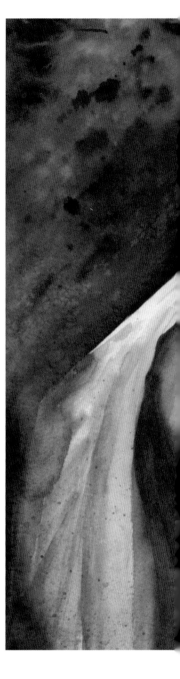

YOU DID THIS FOR ME

Locked in prison
of my own making
Hope was lost;
my heart was breaking
Till you came to set me free
Why would you do this for me?

You did this for me
Spilt precious blood
In Gethsemane
Ravaged by forces within
Pierced by my sorrow and sin

You did this for me
You gave your life
On Calvary
Wounds in these hands that I see
Why would you do this for me?

My child, I love you
These wounds that you see
Are keys to the prison
They'll set you free
Engraved is your name
In my hands and my soul
I'll never forsake you
In me be whole

You did this for me
Broke ev'ry bond
From my chains I'm free
Jesus, my Lord, I love thee
Safe in thy love I will be

Free . . .

You Did This For Me © 2013 by Susan and David Edwards

Who Touched Me by Dianne Johnson Adams

daily life? Do I prioritize His voice over the chaos that surrounds me? Do I really come close and face Him with my full attention? Is He on *my* front row? Am I inclining my ear (see D&C 121:4) to Hear Him?

If I work that hard to hear the noise of the world, can I work a little harder to hear the inspiration of the heavens?

Listening to God Builds Our Relationship with Him and Allows Us to Become like Him

Helen Keller, who was both deaf and blind, purportedly said, "Blindness cuts us off from things, but deafness cuts us off from people." Conversely, careful listening draws us closer to others, strengthening and deepening our relationships.

Listening does the same thing for our relationship with God. But if we choose not to listen to His voice, we choose spiritual deafness to accompany our temporary, veiled blindness.

Fortunately, spiritual deafness does not require expensive hearing aids or invasive cochlear implants to resolve it; it requires only "a broken heart and a

Behold Your Little Ones
by Dan Burr

> *By the power of the Holy Ghost, thoughts come to my mind and feelings to my heart that can help me to see things that are going well and the things that I need to improve and do better.*
>
> —ELDER DAVID A. BEDNAR

contrite spirit" (3 Nephi 9:20). Those are the only assistive hearing devices we need—and the quality of sound they provide is pitch perfect! But here, too, it may take months and even years—nay, a lifetime of practice!—for us to hear and understand with better and better clarity and quality.

One day, I will stand before the Lord and, I hope, "be like him" and, veil lifted, "see him as he is" (Moroni 7:48). To recognize and be like Him on that great day, it will be absolutely necessary for me to have spent my life hearkening to His voice. Seeing Him will be bittersweet, I think, if spiritual deafness means I cannot even understand His voice.

Seeing the Lord Is Not Enough

I do yearn for the day when I will see Him face-to-face. But sight alone falls short of giving me an understanding of God. Throughout the scriptures, hearkening to the voice of the Lord is crucial to real understanding and the real change that can follow. Listening to God is our primary means of experiencing Him during this life!

If we approach Him with love and humility, He will respond to our cries. He yearns to hear us just as we yearn to Hear Him. I am so grateful that this type of communication can never be compromised by a physical limitation.

This essay is modified from chapters in *Hear Him: Listening to the Voice of God in Scriptures and in Our Lives*, Taylor Halverson, Lisa Halverson, and Tyler Griffin (Line of Sight Publishing, 2020). Used with permission.

Made to Move in His Majesty and Power

BY JOSEPH F. BRICKEY

As an artist who treasures both beauty and holiness, I yearn for the divine light that breaks through the material curtains of this physical world, and it thrills me to the core to experience the sacred character of God's spectacular creations. For me, the gospel lens opens my eyes to see the perpetual eclipse of eternal forms behind earthly ones (see D&C 77:2). Seeing the alignment of physical phenomenon with spiritual truth is the impetus of my artistic aspirations, and through it, I feel the majesty of my Maker and the divinity of my own potential.

As a young man, my growing testimony of Joseph Smith's First Vision strengthened my faith that I, too, might have my own witness of God's nature, and I became "desirous also that I might see, and hear, and know of these things, by the power of the Holy Ghost" (1 Nephi 10:17).

Over time, despite my inadequacies, I have found I can still Hear Him on this side of the veil, for "the Spirit enlighteneth every man through the world" (D&C 84:46). Contemplating nature and employing creativity, I believe one can "speak to the earth, and it shall teach thee . . . that the hand of the Lord hath wrought this" (Job 12:8–9), for "the earth [shines] with His glory" (Ezekiel 42:2).

Being an artist affords the frequent opportunity to marvel at God's handiwork, ponder "by whom all things were made which live, and move, and have a being" (D&C 45:1), and realize through the simplest forms of life that "the kingdoms of the world, in all their glory, are not arrayed like one of these" (D&C 84:82). Truly, the eye of faith that looks upon any part of creation "hath seen God moving in his majesty and power" (D&C 88:47).

When my spiritual senses are in tune, I hear His voice echo all around me, for "all things have their likeness, and all things are created and made to bear record of [Him]" (Moses 6:63).

Christic in America by Joseph F. Brickey

The gradual increase of light radiating from the rising sun is like receiving a message from God "line upon line, precept upon precept" (2 Nephi 28:30).

—ELDER DAVID A. BEDNAR

The One Who Returned by Dana Mario Wood

I renew my plea for you to do whatever it takes to increase your spiritual capacity to receive personal revelation. Doing so will help you know how to move ahead with your life, what to do during times of crisis, and how to discern and avoid the temptations and the deceptions of the adversary.

—PRESIDENT RUSSELL M. NELSON

Most especially, as I consider the diversity and endless beauty of the human family, I Hear Him bear "witness with [my] spirit, that we are the children of God" (Romans 8:16). If we can see in the least of His creations "God moving in his majesty and power," we are certainly "eyewitnesses of his majesty" (2 Peter 1:16) as we look upon His children and stand in awe of the incomprehensible marvel that is the human tabernacle, it being the most holy and sacred of His creations, made in His very image and the actual temple of His habitation.

We, as His dear children—and as divinely appointed creators—can especially be made to move in His majesty and power. It is our birthright to not just Hear Him but to also emulate Him (see Ephesians 5:1).

When His covenant people, who are "acquainted with [His] voice" (D&C 84:52), magnify their gifts and fulfill their highest potential, then shall the entire world hear "the voice of his words like the voice of a multitude" (Daniel 10:6), and the Lord "shall utter his voice out of Zion ... and his voice shall be heard among all people" (D&C 133:21).

By such small and simple means can His majesty and power be revealed! In His infinite wisdom, our witness becomes testimony when we "give light to each other in [our] times and in [our] seasons" (D&C 88:44). In this way, **"every man shall hear the fulness of the gospel in his own tongue ... shed forth upon them for the revelation of Jesus Christ"** (D&C 90:11).

Let God Love You

BY WENDY ULRICH

My assumptions were challenged one day more than fifteen years ago in a completely unexpected way. My home office at that time had a large desk, two overstuffed chairs with an ottoman between them, and a large picture window overlooking a grove of trees. I was in the habit of sitting in one of the big chairs by the window to pray, looking at a spot in the sky above the trees as I presented my needs to God, up there in heaven. I had learned to speak freely to God of my desires for His blessings, my concerns for those I love, my struggles and gratitudes and hopes. But on that day I don't recall that I was particularly concerned about anyone, nor was I upset or worried.

I was simply gazing at the distant sky and talking to God as I often did about whatever was on my mind when a still, small voice startled me by talking back. Out of the blue (pretty literally), the question came clearly and distinctly into my mind:

Why do you keep me so far away?

The question stopped me cold—both because it wasn't often that I had such a direct experience of the Spirit speaking words to me and because the question itself caught me completely off guard. Most of my life I had wanted—*longed*, in fact—to feel closer to God.

I had had intimate experiences with God before, close and personal moments of sweet and pure revelation. But here was this question, hanging in the air, and there was God, somewhere up in the sky, waiting for my response.

Not sure what else to do, I took my eyes off the spot up there in the sky, turned my attention to the chair on the other side of the ottoman, and tried to imagine God there instead of up in the clouds. But the oddest thing happened: I just couldn't look. I began to weep uncontrollably. I had the strongest urge to fall down on the floor and sob at His feet. The words of Isaiah came forcefully and meaningfully to my memory and heart, and I understood them in some new place in my soul:

Gentle Touch by Karen Foster

"Woe is me! for I am undone; because I am a man of unclean lips, and I dwell in the midst of a people of unclean lips: for mine eyes have seen the King, the Lord of hosts" (Isaiah 6:5).

Woe, woe indeed! It took several minutes and several attempts before I could so much as raise my face to imagine the face of God so, so close. I thought I would never stop crying, so deep was the reverence that I felt. And when I did, somewhere in my mind He spoke again. Sweetly. Gently. And yet His words pierced my soul:

Why do you keep me so far away?

My heart caught. But He was so close! So close that I almost couldn't breathe for the intensity of that nearness! My weeping broke through again as I tried,

He Is Risen by Eric Boden

Along with the peaceful direction we receive from the Holy Ghost, from time to time, God powerfully and very personally assures each of us that He knows us and loves us and that He is blessing us specifically and openly. Then, in our moments of difficulty, the Savior brings these experiences back into our mind.

—ELDER NEIL L. ANDERSEN

almost painfully, to imagine Him yet closer, sitting on the ottoman only inches from my chair. I had invited God into my room, but now I was allowing Him close enough to touch me with His finger. I felt as if His eyes, though unseen, penetrated my soul. Every instinct of my heart was to run and hide and beg Him not to look at me with such pure eyes. It was not that I felt displeasure or criticism or expectation from Him—not at all. It was just that I felt so known, more known than I have ever felt before. I could not hide. But hiding is what I do!

Nor could I hide from myself in the brightness of that gaze. It was not that I could not stand to see how bad I was. What I could not stand was to see how loved I was, how valued, how known. The very things I had longed for now seemed to burn me as I got so close to them. I sat folded up in my overstuffed chair, barely able to raise my eyes to consider the spot where I was now allowing God to be. I opened my heart a little more to the overwhelming awe and reverence I felt for God. I realized with complete astonishment how utterly true it was that I was the one who had kept Him away, for I obviously could barely, barely tolerate what I was experiencing.

And then, as I felt myself begin to breathe again, I could sense He was about to speak again. I heard within my mind the question:

Why do you keep me so far away?

The question now felt truly unbearable. The only way God could come any closer would be for Him to put His arms around me, His face next to my face, His eyes too close to possibly evade. How, how could I let the God of heaven love me that much? And yet there He was, humbly waiting on my permission, my willingness to receive Him.

Security by David Bowman

I let God hold me that day. With the eyes of my soul, I saw Him step out of His big world and into my small world and embrace me with a love so knowing and so real that I have no words with which to describe it. On that day, I felt as if I were standing in a searing flame more real than anything else in the entire world.

So really—why *do* we keep God so far away?

Perhaps because we've learned through hard experience that relationships—even the ones we think we want—are dangerous. Fortunately, they are also the very best things in our lives.

This essay is modified from *Let God Love You* by Wendy Ulrich, 2016 © Deseret Book Company. Used with permission.

The Invitation by Jenedy Paige

Acting on First Promptings

BY ERIC D. RICHARDS

"We must be confident in our *first* promptings. Sometimes we wonder if we are feeling a spiritual impression or if it is just our own thoughts. When we begin to second-guess, even third-guess . . . we are dismissing the Spirit" (Ronald A. Rasband, "Let the Holy Spirit Guide," *Ensign*, May 2017; emphasis added).

One Fold One Shepherd
by Garth Oborn

Enlightenment by Judy Cooley

My Time Is at Hand by Nathan Pinnock

These words from Elder Ronald A. Rasband will forever be in my heart! The principle of seeking to act on first promptings has helped me Hear Him in amazing new ways.

I cannot think of anything more important in this day than having the promise that I can hear Him, that I can receive His guidance, His reassurance, and His protection in my life. Hearing Him is not complicated but is spiritually demanding and takes time.

—ELDER DAVID A. BEDNAR

The idea of acting on first promptings is not new doctrine. Nearly 200 years ago, the Prophet Joseph taught that if we listen to the first prompting, we will be right nine times out of ten (see Truman G. Madsen, *Joseph Smith the Prophet*, [Salt Lake City: Deseret Book, 1989], 103). Sounds wonderful, doesn't it? To know with 90-percent certainty that an impression came directly from heaven and not from our own thoughts?[1] But for most of us, we struggle with recognizing the first prompting when it comes.[2]

Adding another factor, since nine out of ten first promptings are from the Holy Ghost, our second impressions may then be from the adversary in his efforts to thwart revelation. His goal is always to talk us out of following promptings.[3] It seems that he loves to play the second fiddle of confusion by sowing doubt and second-guesses.

So how do we become better at this process of recognizing and acting on first promptings? Prayer is paramount in this effort. Years ago, during a time when I was earnestly seeking to be more in tune and have more opportunities to recognize my own first promptings, my family and I were watching the movie *War Room*. In the film, Miss Clara uses her closet for an amazing approach to her daily prayers. Touched by this film, I decided to use a similar method. Each day, I use the closet in our master bedroom for my personal prayers and bring with me a printed list of things I want to pray for. It has helped me

---

1 Sister Camilla Kimball, wife of the prophet Spencer W. Kimball, said simply: "Never suppress a generous thought" (quoted by Sister Julie B. Beck, "Relief Society: A Sacred Work"). Acting quickly and courageously on first impressions will lead us to do many good things and will give us many opportunities to bless other people!

2 First promptings can be compared to the chimes we often hear on our cell phones that notify us of calls, updates, or text messages. Loren Dalton gave an excellent talk about this process at the LDS Business College devotional on May 21, 2019, called "You Are Receiving Revelation . . . Now Act on It!"

3 Revelation takes skill and practice. President James E. Faust explained that years ago, in order to tune into a radio station, he had to scratch a tiny wire over the top of bumpy crystals to receive a signal. He said that if he was just one millimeter off, he would lose the signal and only hear static. However, over time, with patience and with a steady hand, he was able to tune into the station ("Did You Get the Right Message?," *Ensign*, May 2004). We must learn to "tune in" to be able to hear our sacred first impressions.

recognize first promptings more often and has increased my courage to reject the second thoughts that try to dissuade me from acting on revelation. Here are my printed prompts that I look at to guide me as I pray each morning:

Express gratitude: What things am I most grateful for today?

Pray for each member of my immediate family.

Pray for members of my extended family.

Pray for my friends.

Pray for my neighbors.

Pray for my coworkers.

Pray for events I read about in the news.

Pray for my bosses and leaders.

Ask for missionary opportunities.

Ask: "Who can I be a blessing to today?" Help guide me to them.

Prince of Peace
by Carly White

Ask: "Help me recognize my first promptings and have the courage to act on them."

Each night as I say my evening prayer, I review my day with Heavenly Father based on a statement from Elder David A. Bednar:

> At the end of our day, we kneel again and report back to our Father. We review the events of the day and express heartfelt thanks for the blessings and the help we received. We repent and, with the assistance of the Spirit of the Lord, identify ways we can do and become better tomorrow. Thus our evening prayer builds upon and is a continuation of our morning prayer . . . . Morning and evening prayers—and all of the prayers in between—are not unrelated, discrete events . . . . This is in part how we fulfill the scriptural admonition to "pray always" (David A. Bednar. "Pray Always," *Ensign*, Nov. 2008).

Reflecting on and reviewing my day each night in prayer has helped me hear the voice of the Spirit and His first promptings more often in my life.

May heaven bless you as you seek to recognize first promptings. Have the courage and clarity of mind to recognize and also reject contrary thoughts when they come to your mind trying to derail your revelation.[4] As you seek to Hear

4 See "Boxing the Lord in: and Other Ways We Hinder Revelation" by Stephen and Michelle Hunsaker.

The Lamb of God by Ken Spencer

Jesus and the Angry Babies by Brian Kershisnik

Peace in Christ by Tausha Schumann

Jesus Washing Disciples' Feet
by Sally Bigelow Rydalch

Him, consider reevaluating your approach to prayer and look to transform that practice into a revelatory moment each day. You can have "revelations daily" (Helaman 11:23), even hour by hour and moment by moment. The more we seek for first promptings as part of our day, the more we will feel heaven's guidance. Let us strive to remove the barriers to our first promptings and Hear Him more often as we begin and end our day with meaningful prayer.

I testify the Lord will magnify every small effort. The Holy Ghost will prompt us to know what to say and do. Such attempts may require us to step out of our comfort zone, but we can be assured that the Lord will help our light shine.

—SISTER BONNIE H. CORDON

I have not always understood how to hear the Lord's voice and enjoy taking the sacrament in my life. When I heard L. Tom Perry's final advice to Church members, that changed for me. Three days before President Perry passed away, President Oaks and Ballard visited him. President Perry said, "[I wish I] could get every member of the Church to go and partake of the sacrament, and when they took the bread, they'd ask themselves, 'Who am I? What am I doing? How am I living? Where am I going? What should I be accomplishing?' as they renew their covenants with the Lord." He finished, "The minute they'd pick up the bread, something [would] happen."

President Perry's advice helped me understand how to ponder my worth and receive direction. I used to dread the sacrament because I would think about all my sins from the preceding week. I felt guilty and disappointed in myself. I made the Savior suffer again and I was not sure which sin to focus on the next week. President Perry's advice changed the sacrament into a delight for me.

First, I would ask, "Who am I?" and then listen. One week I heard the Spirit whisper, "You're a sunflower," or another week it was, "You are mine." I felt unconditional love, much like the love a Father would have for his child. Then I would ask, "What should I do?" One week I heard the word "languid." I did not know what the word meant so when I arrived home, I looked it up in the dictionary. Languid meant slow, relaxed, and peaceful. That week I was hosting a community event which I was worried about. Usually when I am under a lot of stress, I will feel irritable and lose my temper. God told me to work slow and steady and I did not lose my temper as much as usual! Everything came together well. A friend showed up at the last second to help put together the platter I was supposed to bring and I got to the event on time! Most importantly, I was thankful for God's direction because He knew just the advice I needed to have a peaceful week. I am grateful I get to Hear Him.

—KRYSTAL MELDRUM

Joseph's First Prayer by Krystal Meldrum

My Peace I Give unto You by Beki Tobiasson

Tuning My Heart to Hear Him

BY JANICE KAPP
PERRY

I have been writing gospel hymns for the past couple of decades with President David B. Larsen of the Dallas East Stake, who is a skilled lyricist and lover of art and music related to gospel themes. Many times, we have written hymns for occasions in his stake or mine, but for the last decade, we have felt a strong urge to write new hymns based solely on the sermons of the First Presidency and Quorum of the Twelve Apostles, as well as those from the sisters in the auxiliary presidencies. We hoped our hymns would be a second witness to their messages.

With our prophet's eloquent and timely counsel to the Saints of our day to strive with all our hearts to Hear Him, we are all tuning our spirits to hear and obey His counsel!

Many have been writing prose, poetry, and music that will aid us in our quest to Hear Him, and President Larsen and I have been no different. We have felt

Light from Above by Brian Call

The Good Shepherd by Miles R. Woods

The hymns that I love the most focus on the restoration and teach powerful doctrinal lessons. And in those messages, in both the music and the lyrics, you can "Hear Him." For me, music often is a channel for the voice of the Lord.

—ELDER DAVID A. BEDNAR

a strong prompting while writing hymns inspired by our April 2020 conference to put our hearts and souls into a hymn based on President Nelson's counsel to Hear Him.

For this particular song, my collaborator wrote the beautiful text and sent it to me to add the music.

I always pray for the Spirit's influence when I begin to write a hymn, but when I looked at my first draft, I felt that I had failed to capture the power of President Nelson's message. Disappointed, I tore up the music and waited until the next morning to try again. This time, instead of bowing my head at my piano bench to ask for the Spirit's influence in my writing, I found time to be alone in my bedroom, then knelt by my bedside and poured out my heart to the Lord, asking Him to please make me equal to the task of writing this important hymn. I remembered the Lord's chastisement of Oliver Cowdery for "taking no thought but to ask" and realized that was what I had done initially. I pled to the depth of my soul for the Lord to help me write this hymn because on my own, I had not created a hymn worthy of the prophet's message.

While I was still kneeling, the thought came to me to reread President Larsen's text and I would know what to do. I went to my studio and studied the text with new interest. I could feel the warm guidance of the Spirit begin to flow as I saw a very interesting pattern in the four verses. The first two lines of each verse were a plea from the prophet, even an admonition to Hear Him, and I knew I should write it in a minor key to give strength to the words. Then I noticed that the last two lines of each verse changed in tone completely and told of all the beautiful things that could happen in our lives

The Body of Christ by Caitlin Connolly

if we would Hear Him. I knew that going into a major key could convey this new feeling beautifully!

I could not wait to sit at the piano and write, this time with excitement and tears on my cheeks, having received instruction from the Spirit to guide me. When it was done and I played through it, I knew it was right and sent it to President Larsen. His response confirmed that I had indeed heard the Spirit's prompting, as I'm sure he had as he'd written the text.

My thank-you prayer was heartfelt!

The Creation by Sabrina Squires

We do not know when the Savior will return, but this we do know. We must be prepared in heart and mind, worthy to receive Him, and honored to be part of all that was prophesied so long ago.

—ELDER RONALD A. RASBAND

As He Ponders by Rob Kirby

Hear Him

Inspired by the General Conference remarks of President Russell M. Nelson
April 2020

Words by
David B. Larsen

Music by
Janice Kapp Perry

1. Will you lis-ten to the voice of the Liv-ing Christ when from heav'n He clear - ly calls? Will you
lis-ten to the words of the Ris-en Lord as He speaks thru right-eous seers Who will
lis-ten to the voice of the Lamb of God when un - right-eous ness a - bounds— When the
lis-ten to the voice of the Son of Man in whom Fa - ther is well pleased? Will you

choose to hear His gen - tle words as He warns and watch-es all? As you
point the straight and nar - row way when the storms of life ap - pear. As you
wick - ed shall call e - vil good and with reck - less pride are crowned. As you
feast up - on the words He speaks, will you heark - en and be - lieve? As you

do, pure in - spi - ra - tion and His mir - a - cles be - gin, For the
do, you'll soon find com - fort as He calms the rag - ing winds And the
do, the Spir - it's pow - er will send faith where doubt had been And the
do, His words will lift you and will change you from with - in, And you'll

Lord will safe - ly guide you as you heed these words, "Hear Him". 2. Will you
Mas - ter will stand with you as you heed these words, "Hear Him" 3. Will you
Sav - ior's love will lead you As you heed these words, "Hear Him!" 4. Will you
gain a more sure wit - ness As you heed these words, "Hear Him."

Copyright © 2020 by David B. Larsen and Janice Kapp Perry
Copying permitted for incidental non-commercial use in home and church.

Art Credits

t though my feelings were deep and often poignant, still I kept myself aloof from all these par

I became somewhat partial to the Methodist sect, and I felt some desire to be united with them;

n young as I was, and so unacquainted with men and things, to come to any certain conclusion w

ans were most decided against the Baptists and Methodists, and used all the powers of both reaso

hand, the Baptists and Methodists in their turn were equally zealous in endeavoring to establish th

? Who of all these parties are right; or, are they all wrong together? If any one of them be arig

I was one day reading the Epistle of James, first chapter and fifth verse, which reads: If any

ll be given him.

time to mine. It seemed to enter with great force into every feeling of my heart. I reflected on

know, and unless I could get more wisdom than I then had, I would never know; for the teach

nfidence in settling the question by an appeal to the Bible.

ust do as James directs, that is, ask of God. I at length came to the determination to "ask of Go

I might venture.

ttempt. It was on the morning of a beautiful, clear day, early in the spring of eighteen hundred a

I had never as yet made the attempt to pray vocally.

nd finding myself alone, I kneeled down and began to offer up the desires of my heart to God.

had such an astonishing influence over me as to bind my tongue so that I could not speak. Thi

seized upon me, and at the very moment when I was ready to sink into despair and abandon myse

who had such marvelous power as I had never before felt in any being—just at this moment of gr

dually until it fell upon me.

the light rested upon me I saw two Personages, whose brightness and glory defy all descripti

other—This is My Beloved Son. Hear Him!

During this time of great excitement my mind was called up to serious reflection and great uneasines

ugh I attended their several meetings as often as occasion would permit. In process of time my

reat were the confusion and astrife among the different denominations, that it was impossible for a

bright and who was wrong.

My mind at times was greatly excited, the cry and tumult were so great and incessant. The Presb

sophistry to prove their errors, or, at least, to make the people think they were in error. On the o

tenets and disprove all others.

In the midst of this war of words and tumult of opinions, I often said to myself: What is to be

ich is it, and how shall I know it.

While I was laboring under the extreme difficulties caused by the contests of these parties of religion

lack wisdom, let him ask of God, that giveth to all men liberally, and upbraideth not; and it

Never did any passage of ascripture come with more power to the heart of man than this did at

in and again, knowing that if any person needed wisdom from God, I did; for how to act I did

religion of the different sects understood the same passages of scripture so differently as to destroy a

At length I came to the conclusion that I must either remain in darkness and confusion, or else

cluding that if he gave wisdom to them that lacked wisdom, and would give liberally, and not up

So, in accordance with this, my determination to ask of God, I retired to the woods to make

nty. It was the first time in my life that I had made such an attempt, for amidst all my anxie

After I had retired to the place where I had previously designed to go, having looked around

d scarcely done so, when immediately I was aseized upon by some power which entirely overcame me

rkness gathered around me, and it seemed to me for a time as if I were doomed to sudden destruction

But, exerting all my powers to acall upon God to deliver me out of the power of this enemy whic

o destruction—not to an imaginary ruin, but to the power of some actual being from the unseen

rm, I saw a pillar of light exactly over my head, above the brightness of the sun, which descende

It no sooner appeared than I found myself adelivered from the enemy which held me bound. W

nding above me in the air. One of them spake unto me, calling me by name and said, pointing to